The Transition to Adulthood and Family Relations

The Transition to Adulthood and Family Relations

An Intergenerational Perspective

Eugenia Scabini, Elena Marta and Margherita Lanz

Ψ **Psychology Press**
Taylor & Francis Group

HOVE AND NEW YORK

First published 2006 by Psychology Press,
27 Church Road, Hove, East Sussex BN3 2FA

Simultaneously published in the USA and Canada
by Psychology Press
270 Madison Avenue, New York NY 10016

*Psychology Press is an imprint of the Taylor & Francis Group, an
informa business*

© 2006 Psychology Press for the United Kingdom

Typeset in Times by Garfield Morgan, Mumbles, Swansea
Printed and bound in Great Britain by MPG Books Ltd, Bodmin,
Cornwall
Cover design by Jim Wilkie

The publisher makes no representation, express or implied, with
regard to the accuracy of the information contained in this book and
cannot accept any legal responsibility or liability for any errors or
omissions that may be made.

This publication has been produced with paper manufactured to strict
environmental standards and with pulp derived from sustainable
forests.

British Library Cataloguing in Publication Data
A catalogue record for this book is available from the British Library

Library of Congress Cataloging-in-Publication Data

Scabini, Eugenia.
    The transition to adulthood and family relations : an
intergenerational approach / Eugenia Scabini, Elena Marta and
Margherita Lanz.
        p. cm.
    Includes bibliographical references and index.
    ISBN 1-84169-380-4 (hardcover)
    1. Parent and teenager. 2. Parent and adult child. 3. Teenagers–
Family relationships. 4. Young adults–Family relationships.
5. Adulthood. 6. Family. 7. Intergenerational relations. I. Marta,
Elena. II. Lanz, Margherita. III. Title.
    HQ799.15.S32 2005
    306.874–dc22

                                                        2005035830

ISBN10: 1-84169-380-4 (hbk)
ISBN13: 978-1-84169-380-4 (hbk)

To Sandy Jackson

Contents

Series preface

In the eyes of the mass media and in the minds of many adults, adolescents are often portrayed in largely negative terms, focusing on features such as their noisy and exuberant social behaviour, teenage gangs and their often violent, anti-social activities, teenage pregnancy, drinking, smoking drug-taking, anti-school attitudes and disagreements with parents.

Such portrayals are painted as if they were typical of what most, if not all, adolescents do, and, accordingly, regarded as a justification for adult society to consider the teenage years as a problem period in human development and adolescents as a problem for society.

For much of the 20th century, this popular, stereotypic picture was supported by what was written by social scientists in books and other publications, which presented adolescence as a period of "storm and stress". Adolescence was seen as a period of turbulence, inner turmoil and confusion, characterised by conflicts with parents, teachers and other authority figures.

Over the last three decades of the 20th century important theoretical changes began to emerge. Psychologists began to question the "storm and stress" perspective and to provide evidence that this developmental pattern was neither a typical nor a necessary part of adolescence. In parallel with this, a less problem-centred approach to thinking about adolescence began to emerge: an approach which emphasized processes of change and adjustment which young people undergo in responding to the varied tasks and transitions which they face. An increasing number of books and articles on adolescence began to appear which differed markedly from earlier publications in emphasis and orientation. In contrast to the clinical perspective, this new work was based on a more empirical approach and focused upon a variety of different aspects of adolescent development. Further, longitudinal assessments over large time spans basically support the idea of a more gradual change leading to an overall positive outcome. Such publications stimulated further interest in adolescence as an area of study and in doing so started a process which led on to the emergence of research on adolescence as one of the most active fields in developmental psychological research. As a result, discussion of many aspects of adolescence has become a prominent feature of developmental conferences and scientific journals in Europe and elsewhere.

However, times change. The early years of the new millennium have seen technological innovations, global risks from terrorism and demographic shifts occurring in most countries of the world. For example, there are now as many people over the age of sixty-five years as there are teenagers in most of the world's societies. Macrosocial changes such as growing up in a context of ethnic diversity and living in single-parent families are increasingly experienced by adolescents in Western industrialized countries.

Further, as the new millennium advances psychology now takes a more positive view of human development, seeing changes and transitions as challenges within the developmental progress of young people, in society generally, *vis-à-vis* cultural and technological innovations and in relation to other generations.

The European Association for Research on Adolescence (EARA) is an organization which aims to promote and conduct high quality fundamental and applied research on all aspects of adolescent development. Its founder and then President, the late Sandy Jackson, devoted much of his professional life to advancing these aims. Before his death in 2003, he initiated a co-operation with Psychology Press to start this series, "Studies in Adolescent Development", and commissioned and published two books during his editorship. We, the new co-editors, are grateful for Sandy's vision and trust that we can progress the academic and professional interest in adolescence as an area of scholarly study which he initiated.

The present series aims to respond to the recent shifts in the social and ecological environment of adolescents and in the new theoretical perspectives within the social sciences, by providing a range of books, each of which deals in depth with an aspect of current interest within the field of adolescent development.

The co-editors delineate a number of broad topics that require significant attention and invite academics, researchers and professionals to submit book proposals. Each proposal is carefully evaluated by the co-editors for selection in the series. Hence, each book is written by a chosen expert (or experts) in a specific aspect of adolescence and sets out to provide either a clear picture of the research endeavours which are currently serving to extend the boundaries of our knowledge and understanding of the field, or an insightful theoretical perspective of adolescent development.

Each book in the series represents a step towards the fulfilment of this aim. The European Association for Research on Adolescence is grateful to Psychology Press for all that it has done in developing and promoting the series and for assisting EARA in extending knowledge and understanding of the many aspects of adolescent development in a rapidly changing and challenging world.

Professors Leo B. Hendry, Marion Kloep & Inge Seiffge-Krenke
Series Editors

Introduction

Transitions are ever-present phenomena, pervasive across all forms of life (Ruble & Seidman, 1996). The study of transitions has been of major interest to social researchers because they are often times of upheaval, affecting self-definition and interpersonal relationships. Of particular attraction to social scientists are the changes that accompany major life transitions, such as puberty, beginning a job, and marriage. Whereas in archaic societies most transitions took place by discrete "leaps" and were accompanied by veritable "rites of passage" that signalled a collective wish to mark the passage to a new condition, in modern contemporary society transitions are represented more and more often as being individual, relatively undefined (with respect to both modalities and timing), negotiable, little ritualized, and with ample margins of choice. An automatic passage has been thus transformed into a *path of transition*, with its own processes and timing. The extension of the life stage spanning the transition from childhood to adulthood is an increasingly common phenomenon in European countries (Cavalli & Galland, 1993) and in the US. This temporal extension is causing a prolongation of adolescence, and is giving rise to a new phase in the life cycle called post-adolescence, or young adulthood (Sherrod, Haggerty & Featherman, 1993). The transition to adulthood is therefore assuming new features. It is no longer a short span of time made up of precise steps, but a long transition characterized by numerous microtransitions (Breunlin, 1988) beginning in late adolescence. On closer scrutiny, the transition to adult life takes the form of a double transition, from the adolescent phase to that of the young adult and from this to the phase of full adulthood. These are not two well-defined transitions, however: rather, the first has the characteristics of a preparatory phase (microtransition) for the true transition that the young person will complete in the next phase (macrotransition). In the preparatory phase, the foundations are laid and the conditions created that will either promote or inhibit the passage to the condition of adulthood (Scabini & Cigoli, 2000). In this we find ourselves in an opposite position to primitive societies, where the process has been condensed to a rapid, highly ritualized "leap" featuring rites of passage that unambiguously define both the transition to adulthood and the impossibility of reverting to the previous situation. However, we are also in a different situation from that of our own recent past, when the transition was clearly mapped out by well-defined markers that occurred in a clear sequence: finishing school, entering the labour market, getting married. Depending on social timing, there was a certain time span in which these tasks could be carried out, particularly for women, for whom the accepted range of time for marrying was quite restricted. The ordering of these markers has now been altered by a modern life style that increasingly allows previously made choices to be revised and reversed, with the result that the most widespread model is now one of experimentation and reversibility (Sciolla, 1993). In short, the transition to adulthood is progressively breaking down into a sequence of individual (Hurrelmann & Engel, 1989) transitory states based on a variety of social and temporal models. Young people can now choose when to make the transition. The slowing down of the transition to adulthood has given more value and more influential power to the family of origin during a period of the life cycle in which, in past decades, it has tended to play only a minor role. The transition to adulthood either occurs within the family of origin or depends on the family of origin for its successful outcome. In other words, the transition to adulthood is a "joint enterprise" of both children and parents. Indeed, parents are in some ways actively engaged in this developmental task (Scabini, 1995; Sroufe, 1991; Youniss & Smollar, 1985). The family, with its crucial position at the intersecting point of gender and generational lines, has always carried out this function of sustenance and support for its offspring, but this willingness of families to support their younger members in the long transition to adulthood is a new phenomenon. The slowing down of this transition is possible only because adolescents and young adults can count on their families: unlike in the past, when all the generations in a family had the same access to family resources, today parents are willing to support the younger generations on the "longer road to adulthood" (Arnett, 2004) and to redirect to them a major portion of the family's resources.

Research has demonstrated that parent–child relationships during late adolescence and young adulthood do not necessarily have to be tumultuous or negative. On the contrary, parents continue to be an important source of support in the process of their children establishing a separate identity. In modern European society, beginning from late adolescence, we are now witnessing an essentially peaceful transformation in family relations.

The changes in the form taken by the transition to adulthood in European societies and those regarding the family's role and functions in this phase of the life cycle offer the possibility of a new quality of relationship between parents and adolescents/young adults. The ongoing family may offer excellent opportunities for dialogue, exchange and emotional warmth, as well as an opportunity for young people to fulfil themselves in the personal sphere, but it can also become closed and inward-looking if it breaks generational continuity by discouraging young people from leaving the nest and accepting parenthood. Therefore, the family is both a new resource and a new source of risk. This is the result of the ambiguous relationship between the family and society, and of the opposing behaviours of generations within the family and society.

How does the transition of young people to adulthood manifest itself today in Europe? What are the contours characterizing the family that makes itself available as a resource for its offspring's transition to adulthood? What is the constellation of variables that makes a family into a source of risk? What are the perceptions regarding family relationships held by different generations—parents and children—and by the actors of each generation—father, mother, son, and daughter—involved in this "joint enterprise"? And, more specifically, what are the interactions between dyads of different generations? And between dyads of the same and different gender, i.e., father–son, mother–daughter; father–daughter, mother–son?

This work intends to provide answers to these questions. It is designed to present: (1) the relational–intergenerational perspective to the study of the family and an overview on the transition to adulthood from this perspective; (2) the methodology for the study of the family from the relational–intergenerational perspective; and (3) the results of 15 years of research on parent–child relationships during the transition to adulthood carried out in Italy from an intergenerational perspective. This perspective to research on the family takes into consideration the points of view of each generation—parents and children—regarding family relationships and then compares the two. This involves carrying out a vertical (intergenerational) analysis necessary to a full understanding of the transition, rather than relying solely on a horizontal (intragenerational) perspective. In addition to an analysis based on different generations, the research also investigates the influence of gender on the object in question. Taken together, the totality of these findings will allow us to conduct an analysis by "gender and generation", as recently requested by the European Union (EU) (May, 2000).

This work takes the form of a research monograph on the transition to adulthood in Italy, in as much as it can be considered a nation of southern Europe. The "case of Italy" will also be debated in the light of a comparison with data from the international literature that are used to provide a background for the research, but always with the focus firmly set on the "case" in question.

The volume consists of two parts. The first part presents the theoretical and methodological framework. More specifically, the *first chapter* presents the relational–intergenerational perspective and studies the transition to adulthood from this point of view. The *second chapter* offers an in-depth analysis of the methodology in the area of family research and, more particularly, regarding families with late adolescents and young adults. In the first place, the distinction is made between true "family research", in which each part of the project is constructed keeping in mind the families' point of view, and "family-related research", in which the family is merely inferred or considered as being part of the "background". As suggested by Fisher, Kokes, Ransom, Philips, and Rudd, (1985), in true family research, the techniques adopted for the analysis of data allow us to study the family as a whole.

The second part of the book presents the results of research conducted by the Centre for Family Studies and Research of Milan at the Catholic University over the past 15 years into the family relationships of late adolescents and young adults in that these are phases in which the processes of the transition to adulthood can be best discerned. The *third chapter* focuses on the quality of the parent–child relationship during the transition to adulthood. The *fourth chapter* looks at the connection between family relationships and offspring's risk behaviour, prosocial behaviour and planning for the future. Both chapters pay particular attention to a comparison between the points of view of parents and children and to an analysis of the exchange between generations and genders.

The volume closes with a series of theoretical and methodological reflections regarding research on family relations during the transition to adulthood and with proposals for future research.

Sincere thanks go to Sandy Jackson, who was the first to believe in this book and supported and encouraged it: not forgotten and unforgettable President of the European Association of Research on Adolescence (EARA), avid supporter of research on adolescence and of the "young generations" of researchers.

A thank you to all our colleagues from EARA, with whom we had occasion over the years to measure ourselves and to exchange, from whom we have learned and with whom we have begun a hopefully long journey together in the name of research into this intriguing phase of life.

We feel deeply indebted and grateful to the three referees who have closely read this work and given us valuable suggestions and advice for improving it and making it more accessible.

Finally, many thanks to our colleagues at the Centre for Family Studies and Research at the Catholic University of Milan, with whom we share the everyday joys and difficulties inherent in the fascinating human pursuit that is research.

Acknowledgement

The translation of this book received the financial support of the Catholic University of Milan in 2003 on the basis of an evaluation of the results of the research presented in it.

Part I

The theoretical and methodological background

1   The identity of the family

INTRODUCTION

The family appears to be an easy object to study. Each of us tends to think
that his or her experience of the family can be readily understood by others
whose own family experiences coincide with our own type of family, which
also happens to be the most prevalent type of family in our own historical
period. A historical perspective, based on the long view, immediately belies
this commonly held misconception. Even a cursory reading of the evidence
plainly reveals the difference between the current organization of the so-
called nuclear family, clearly demarcated from relatives and geographic
community, and the premodern family, whose boundaries are extremely
permeable to external influences. In the latter family type, the married
couple, under the husband's authority, was often undifferentiated from
relatives and the community. As Laslett and Wall (1972) clearly demonstrated in their studies on European families, over the centuries we have
seen the demise and resurgence of many types of family (nuclear, without
structure, extended, multiple, complex): the list goes on to include today's
broken families, stepfamilies and immigrant families from various cultures
that, thanks to our global society, find themselves living in proximity to
each other with increasing frequency.

Faced with such a rich variety of family forms, past and present, it is
crucial to answer the following questions: What are the elements that
constitute the family's identity beyond the particular forms it has assumed?
What is the perspective that is best able to fathom its nature?

In the light of these preliminary observations, our first task will be to
acquaint the reader with the theoretical framework and perspective that
direct our efforts to observe and understand the fascinating and complex
world of the family.

How can we define the family? An answer that immediately comes to
mind is that the family is a group. Lewin (1951) says of the group that it is
something different from the sum of its members: it has its own structure,
peculiar aims and particular relations with other groups. Its essence is not
constituted by the similarity or dissimilarity found between its members,

but by their *interdependence*. It can be defined as a dynamic totality. This means that a change in the condition of any of its parts impacts the state of all the others. This definition is well suited to the structural and functional characteristics of the family. Each member of the family exists in reciprocal relationship with the others, influences them and is influenced by them (Levine & Moreland, 1998). More specifically, in early studies of groups, Cooley (1909) had already pointed out that the family is a particular type of group, a *primary* group, since it carries out a fundamental role in building both individual identity and society. Indeed, the family is at the origin of the phenomenon of civilization itself in that it guarantees the generative process in biological, psychological, social, and cultural terms (Murdock, 1949). Many authors have tried to discern the distinctive aspects of the family with respect to other types of group. In particular, the comparison was carried out with artificial groups, which attracted, after Lewin, a good deal of the experimental investigation. This perspective has given us the very concise and expressive definition of the family as a *group with a history* (Olson, 1969). Unfortunately, this dimension of "family history" has not been developed much beyond its initial enunciation and thus the aspects of the "ongoing" intergenerational bond that characterizes families have been left in the background. In later decades, attention was focused on critical aspects of the functioning of the family nucleus, such as cohesion, adaptability, and family competence, giving rise to interesting debates (Beavers & Hampson, 1993; Olson, 1993). Family boundaries (clear versus confused) were analysed within the perimeter of the nuclear family and between the nuclear family and the social context (Walsh, 1993). The exchanges between the family nucleus and the family of origin—that is to say, the history of what came before—were ignored. It is necessary, however, to identify the distinctive aspects of the family starting from the fact that the family is a primary group with a history of preceding bonds and that it, in turn, generates future bonds.

Thus, we define the family as an organization of primary relationships founded upon the difference of gender and the difference between generations and lineages. Its purpose and intrinsic project is generativity (Scabini, 1995). Some clarification of this definition is in order. The term *organization* used by Sroufe and Fleeson (1988) refers to a group and to a system. In fact, as already noted by Buckley (1976), who adopted a sociological perspective, and Haley (1973), from the viewpoint of psychology, the family has an organized structure and an internal hierarchy that permeates the parent–child relationship and, in the past—and even to this day in many cultures—characterizes the marital relationship as well. If the family *organizes relationships*, these are not generic (or just any) relationships but primary relationships that connect and bind the crucial differences of human nature: the differences between genders and generations. These, in turn, give rise to a relational asset—new generations and their upbringing—that are essential to the human community. It is important to be specific about how family bonds are primary. In the family, individuals are bound to each other as human beings over and above the roles they fulfil. The connection of relationship to role is inclusive. Specifically, there are two relational axes within the family: the marital and the parent–child, with the related sibling axis.

The marital relationship is based on *gender difference*. The term "gender" refers to the sociocultural identity of the male and female sexes. Every culture translates sex as a biological fact into a feminine and masculine identity, with roles and functions as well as social and cultural characteristics. The dynamic of connectedness and separateness that distinguishes the life of every group finds in the family its original basis. In the human species, unlike other animals, there is a great variability in the characteristics considered typical of the female and male genders. The family, unlike other groups, is characterized by a specific way of living and constructing gender differences by means of a process that is surely biological, but also relational and social (Crespi, 2004). The family "is" the social and symbolic place in which difference, in particular sexual difference, is believed to be fundamental and, at the same time, constructed (Saraceno, 1988). In particular, gender characterization reflects the individualities of the parents in the family. The family is, therefore, a "gender relationship". The fact that in different cultures expectations and behaviours connected to gender can vary is not in itself problematical for the construction of an individual's identity. What might be considered as risk factors, however, are the extreme differentiation between roles, common in the past (rigid identity), or the excessive similarity of roles, as might happen today (confused identity).

The parent–child relationship implies *difference in generations* and the ensuing responsibility of the older generation towards the next one. The term "parental" includes both one's own parents as well as the network of relatives constituted by relationships with each spouse's family of origin. In other words, it involves both the difference between parents and offspring and the difference between family and lineage, a difference that is lost over time. We can assert, therefore, that the "psychic field" of the family is much vaster than the dual space created by the relationship between parents and offspring or between partners: it is at least trigenerational. The spouses' parents are also the "offspring" of the preceding generations and their *identity* has to do with both the parental and the filial relationship. The purpose and the intrinsic project of the family are summed up in the verb *to generate*. The family does not reproduce individuals: instead, it generates persons, it humanizes that which derives from itself and that within itself is bound together. In human beings, biological heritage is from the beginning embedded in and influenced by the cultural dimension: the goal of procreation is not only the continuation of the species but, by means of biological generation, is also the psychic generation of persons who will carry on and innovate the family and social history. Moreover, the act of generation gives a specific quality to the relationship between the sexes:

through their child, a mother and father come to be bound inextricably together and can never again "leave" the parental relationship (one cannot become an ex-parent or an ex-grandparent). The families of origin are also bound together through the child; a difference of generations is produced together with a bond between lineages that is lost over time. Uniqueness and belonging also characterize the newborn: he or she is able to develop psychically thanks to being "acknowledged" within a relationship of a specific lineage. Each child thus carries in his or her surname the sign of belonging to the family history and in his or her name a sign of uniqueness. The generative bond should be understood in its intergenerational sense, that is, in its double meaning of generating and being generated. It is for this reason that, in order to capture the object "family", one must go beyond a dualistic perspective limited to the examination of the parent–child interaction or, more frequently, the mother–child interaction, and take into consideration multiple generations. Looking at generativity from a relational point of view also means not conceiving of it as a characteristic exclusive to adults: it is something that is received and given, something that others have passed on to us and that we, in turn, will pass on, after having given it our own imprint. Kotre (Kotre, 1984; Kotre & Kotre, 1998) and Snarey (1998) have identified different types of generativity:

- *Biological* generativity includes producing a child and providing the care necessary to his/her physical survival and the development of basic trust. Its opposite is the experience of infertility, which indirectly threatens the other forms of generativity as well, because it weakens their premises.
- *Parental* generativity manifests itself in those care-related activities that promote the child's development of its potential in achieving a balance between autonomy, initiative, industriousness, and identity. Parental generativity also consists in passing on to a child the family's values and traditions. It becomes a factor in moral development because the virtue of caring for a child overcomes the inevitable hesitation one experiences when faced with an irreversible commitment, such as the one parents accept with respect to their children.
- *Social* generativity, expressed in the acceptance of responsibility for young people, contributes to the strengthening and continuity of the generations by providing guidance and direction for the growth and wellbeing not only of one's own children but also of other young people who belong to the same generation.

The family has been studied from the perspective of several different approaches: the Family Development Theory, the Family Stress and Coping Theory, the Symbolic-Interactionist Theory, Systems Framework and the

Ecological Framework (Box 1.1, for an overview, see Doherty, Boss, LaRossa, Schumm, & Steinmetz, 1993; Klein & White, 1996). In this work, however, we rely upon the relational–intergenerational perspective (Cigoli & Scabini, forthcoming), in which various aspects of the approaches just mentioned are incorporated and reinterpreted.

Box 1.1

Theories about families

The Family Development Theory: historically, this represents the first systematic attempt to explain the principal predictable changes in the family. This theory was developed in three phases. The first conceptualization of the theory dates to Rowntree (1903) and is characterized by the rise of the idea of the family life cycle. The next phase, worked out by Hill and Duvall (Duvall, 1977; Hill, 1949a, 1949b), is characterized by the theory's systematization. The third and most recent phase reveals an interest in the concept of the life cycle and research instruments (White, 1991) and theorizes family as an enterprise that can be followed across stages of development. It revolves around the idea that families change form and function over the course of their life cycle in an ordered sequence of developmental stages. Every stage of the family life cycle is characterized by the presence of specific developmental tasks related to components of the family either entering or leaving it (for example, marriage, birth . . .). Modern developments of the theory, from the work of McGoldrick, Heiman, and Carter (1993a, 1993b), besides emphasizing the intergenerational implications of the life cycle, have effected a reconnection between the family and the social environment in which it lives.

The Family Stress and Coping Theory: initially developed as an attempt to study the effects produced by unforeseen changes within the family (for example, the premature death of a member) or outside it (for example, economic crises), over time, it approached—and was integrated into—developmental theory. In the theoretical discussion of Hill (1949a, 1949b) and later, Burr (1973), McCubbin and Patterson (1981), the family is understood as a system continually subjected to demands that take the form of stressors or strains, which the family counters with its own capacities in terms of resources and coping or adaptive behaviours. According to these authors, every family passes, over the course of time, through repeated cycles characterized by phases of functioning and adaptation interspersed with family crises.

The Symbolic-Interactionist Theory: this theory is rooted in the thought of Charles Pierce, William James, John Dewey and, above all, George Herbert Mead, who argued that human actions can be understood only in relation to language, society, and culture and that, by sharing common symbols, humans can adapt to and survive in their environment. The general focus of symbolic interactionism can be summarized as the acquisition and generation of meaning assigned by persons to actions and to the context in which they live. One of the concepts at the basis of this theory is that of role, with respect to which the dimension of the expectations that both actor and others have about the performance of the role, role strain and role conflict have been studied with particular emphasis. The theory has been used to understand diverse aspects of family functioning: the family domain contains a sense of shared history and future and a sense of biography. The enhancement theory and the concept of role overload (Marks, 1977) have their roots in this theoretical framework.

The Systems Framework: this interdisciplinary perspective was born in the 1940s and has antireductionist and antisectoral intentions. It takes into consideration the complexity of living organisms (von Bertalanffy & Rapoport, 1960), shedding light on the significant relationships between their parts and functions and between the organisms themselves and their surrounding environments (supersystems). This theory's presupposition is that the family is a system and in a system all the parts are interconnected; thus, understanding is only possible by viewing the whole. Boundaries, rules of transformation, feedback, subsystems, variety and equilibrium are considered in each system. The application of the systemic principles to therapeutic practice conceives of the individual's symptom as a difficulty of the entire family system, even if today therapeutic practice is no longer anchored to intervention *vis-à-vis* the family as whole.

The Ecological Framework: the most basic notion in the ecological framework is adaptation: for example, a family can adapt to changing social and economic conditions. Having originated within the field of biology, this framework has been applied to various environments—one of which is the family—with the idea that individuals and groups are both biological and social in nature. In this framework, the family is considered as a social organization embedded in a larger kinship network (Hawley, 1986). It occupies a niche in society by providing for the sustenance and nurturance of its components and by providing to society the reproduction of economic and social organizations. In short, according to this perspective, the individual grows and adapts through interchanges with his or her immediate ecosystem (the family) and more distant environments, such as school (Bronfenbrenner, 1979).

THE RELATIONAL DIMENSION

In our definition of the family we used the term "relationship". It is worth elaborating on this terminology. The concept of relationship has enjoyed considerable success in the field of psychology in recent decades. We have seen a laborious but progressive consolidation of theoretical perspectives that make the idea of relationship the central interpretative key for psychosocial phenomena. We might mention, for example, the recent developments in the study of one of social psychology's principal topics, that of self and identity. The statement that a relational self exists, which is to say, a representation of self connected to a person's significant relationships, is by now commonly accepted. Hinde, Finkenauer, and Auhagen (2001) remind us that the concept we have of ourselves impacts the relationships we are involved in and, vice versa, that relationships modify and influence what we think of ourselves. Interest in the concept of relationship has also been translated into the development of a specific field of investigation, that of personal or close relationships. This research has taken as its object personal and intimate relationships that extend over a person's lifetime and that can be considered a sort of extension of family relationships (Duck, 1988, 1997). Attachment theory, which has enjoyed so much success in theoretical discussions and research, has also given priority to a primary relationship, that between the mother and her son or daughter.

What do we mean by relationship? In the relational–intergenerational perspective, the concept of relationship has to do with that which binds people together: it always has an intergenerational dimension. As we have already pointed out, not only the child but also the adult spouse and/or parent is always a son or daughter and this "historical" bond contributes to the definition of one's identity and influences interactions taking place in the present. It should be noted, however, that very often in the literature on psychology the term relationship is used interchangeably with interaction. Our perspective distinguish and connect interaction and relationship: these are two different analytical levels, each able to stand on its own. The widely adopted interactive approach does not distinguish between interaction and relationship, to the extent that relationship "collapses" into interaction. Our perspective, on the contrary, is multilevel. Specifically, it considers that interaction is an indispensable part of any observation of the family and that it, in turn, allows one to access the relational level. Interaction is the tangible substance of family life and is therefore the obligatory starting point for any family analysis. Interaction indicates "action between participants" in the sense of whatever can be observed in the here and now, which is to say, the exchanges and communication that occur in a family's everyday life. Its essence can be found in whatever individuals build through their shared everyday action. The semantic field of interaction is dominated by space and by the co-construction of meanings and joint actions, while its temporal aspect focuses on the present and on sequence. However, even if this level of analysis is a necessary starting point, we cannot stop here but must continue on to a higher level. This is the relational level, to which the interactive level is subordinated. Family relationships cannot be reduced to a mere sequence of observable, reciprocal actions, which are, within limits, also measurable. Indeed, "although an interaction could be defined as having one meaning or 'focus', a relationship is likely to have many, each superordinated to those of numerous types of interactions" (Hinde, 1997, p. 38). Family relationships point to something other than what is observed: they point to a bond that precedes the interaction in progress and constitutes its meaningful context. A relationship cannot be observed in the same way that we observe an interaction: it can only be inferred. A family's everyday interactions can be understood only if one considers that the family members who interact with each other are previously bound to each other because they have common origins and common affiliations. They are connected and bound to the history of the generations from which they descend and which have physically and psychically generated them. Moreover, the history of a family's generations is also cultural and societal history, since the family is a living, social organization. The family relationships become particularly accessible during a family's transitions (the transition to parenthood, to adult life, to divorce, etc.), which reveal the strengths and weaknesses of family bonds. The actions and the verbal and non-verbal exchanges that family members engage in among themselves (interactive level) convey superordinated meanings summed up in the expression "value of the bond". This is the comprehensive meaning of the family bond and of the various types of bonds. We know that interactions taking place in the present, as well as the expectations and experiences of the past, contribute to determining this comprehensive meaning. The marital or parental relationship may be constructed or co-constructed and can be modified, but it is always based on a cognitive and ethical-affective, mental and value-imbued inheritance passed on by and assimilated in one's own family of origin and its culture of belonging. It is only through the culture in which the family is immersed and that it shares with other social groups—and also through its specific intergenerational history that the new couple must acknowledge and negotiate—that families can access the symbolic reference. When a researcher adopts a relational perspective, he or she seeks to reconstruct, based on the accounts of family members, a comprehensive story of the family experience, weaving together the different parts of the single relationships established by each family member. The quality of the bonds between family members and the type of exchanges between generations are the elements specific to the relational level. Therefore, unlike interaction that focuses on the present, relationships are long term: they thrive on the connection between past, present and future. Table 1.1 synthesises the preceding points.

THE SYMBOLIC DIMENSION: AFFECTIVE AND ETHICAL QUALITIES

Family relations are permeated and sustained by manifest and latent meanings that have a symbolic quality. We use the term "symbolic" in the same way that it is used in anthropology and, more recently, in cultural psychology (Cole, 1996; Mantovani, 2000) and that is, as a *latent meaning structure*. This structure derives from the convergence of basic qualities that

Table 1.1 Characteristics of the analytical levels pertaining to the family

	Interactive level	*Relational level*
Specifics	Analysis of interactions between spouses, siblings, and between parents and offspring	Analysis of the quality of bonds between spouses, siblings, generations
Area of investigation	Everyday routines, sequence of typical situations	Family transitions, ceremonies and rituals, processes of identity transformation
Timing	Present	Connection between past, present and future

characterize family bonds. These are expressed in the literature by various constructs, such as intimacy, emotions, support, commitment, and control, but can all be seen to fall into the categories of affective and ethical factors. The family is indeed the context *par excellence* in which affective qualities and responsibility towards others are generated, whether with respect to the child that one cares for or the man or woman to whom one commits oneself. The meaning of the family bond is therefore two orders of factors, affective and ethical. Trust[1] and hope are prototypes of the affective quality, along with openness and the credit one gives to the other; loyalty and justice are prototypes of the ethical quality[2] (Figure 1.1).

For Erickson, trust and hope are at the core of an individual's perspective, and more generally, attachment theory identifies the bond of trust between mother and child as providing a solid foundation for development. According to Meltzer and Harris (1983), infusing hope and breeding trust are the family's basic objectives with respect to the new generations. Mistrust and despair result when families fail to engender trust and hope. According to the authors' theory, the tension between these feelings (trust–mistrust; hope–despair) are the *core of family emotional exchanges*. Loyalty and justice are prototypes of the ethical quality: Boszormenyi-Nagy and Spark (1973), drawing on the phenomenology of the philosopher Martin Buber, have further developed these aspects. There is inscribed in man an order of multipersonal justice: every act of justice or injustice has psychological effects on the recipient, but also has consequences for posterity and for the intergenerational legacy. These qualities coexist with their opposite, to some extent: a certain degree of lack of trust and injustice as well as prevarication is present in every family. From a symbolic point of view, we may correlate the affective pole with the *maternal* function (*matris-munus*), which consists in the giving of life and warmth, and the ethical pole with the *paternal* function (*patris-munus*), in the sense of conferring belonging and transmitting material and moral heredity. The expression "to

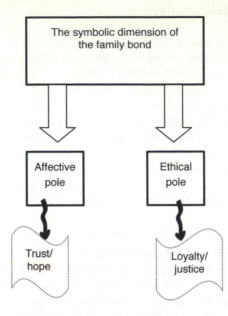

Figure 1.1 The symbolic dimension of the family bond.

care for", typical of family-oriented semantics, expresses both poles, not split between but rather shared by feminine and masculine figures. To care for someone refers to nurturing that is both affective and moral in nature, and both act to sustain the family bond. The family's health derives from the joint and hopefully balanced presence of these two poles. Moreover, the dialectic between affective and ethical aspects takes on specific characteristics in relation to the social context and cultural climate in which the family lives. Whereas in past societies the normative aspect was very strong and the affective element was of secondary importance, our society has witnessed an opposite tendency. Both in the marital and the parental relationship there has been a progressive weakening of the value given to the ethical dimension and a parallel appreciation in the value accorded to the affective dimension, especially with respect to its expressive and emotional connotations. The way in which the marital bond is understood in our society is emblematic of this trend. The ethical aspect takes second stage to affective aspects, often understood in the weak sense of "feelings". Today's couple tends to look to itself for direction, culturally disengaging from any reference to preceding generations and institutional constraints. But even the parent–child relationship is analysed and viewed mostly from the perspective of its affective aspects of understanding, dialogue and agreement rather than referring, as in the past, to normative elements and "rules of behaviour". As we shall see, the research also reflects this strong emphasis on affective constructs.

The process of related distinction

Many authors have emphasized that the fundamental process that the family undergoes makes it possible to bring together the tendency of the system towards unity and maintaining bonds—that is to say, towards connectedness—and the opposite push towards differentiation and autonomy—that is to say, towards separateness. In other words, family functioning is played out in the dialectic between belonging and autonomy. We call this process *related distinction*. The psychological literature has dealt at length with the process of individuation and differentiation (Sabatelli & Mazor, 1985). The former is understood to be an individual process that allows the adolescent to move from a position of infantile dependence on parental figures to a position of autonomy. The latter is more properly a process that involves the family system and that has to do with the capacity of family members to adjust the psychological distances between themselves, allowing for moments of closeness and distance (Anderson & Sabatelli, 1992; Cooper, Grotevant, & Condon, 1983). This second process acts according to an interactive and spatial perspective, as clearly indicated by the metaphor's reference to the adjustment/negotiation of interpersonal distances and boundaries. Its advantage consists in shifting attention from an individual perspective typical of the process of individuation (it is the single individual who separates and asserts his or her individuality) to a group-systemic perspective, focused on interactive patterns where the level of conflict and degree of parental intrusiveness play a key role. Its limitation is that it does not render the relational–intergenerational aspect that is so characteristic of the family. An attempt to remedy this situation was carried out by Stierlin (1974) when he used the expression "related individuation", thus emphasizing the reciprocal influence or relationship between the parents' capacity to tolerate the pain of detachment and the capacity of their offspring to assume an autonomous and responsible role.

Our conception clearly gives centre stage to a relational–intergenerational perspective and joins together the spatiality of interaction with the verticality of relationship. We have called this process *related distinction* to highlight both the intergenerational reciprocity-connection of the process and the relationship between connectedness and separateness that originates the distinction. The term "distinction" is used here in accordance with the tradition of social psychology with regard to identity construction. In particular, we are thinking of the Optimal Distinctiveness Theory formulated by Brewer (1991), who emphasizes that social identity is the product of the tension between the need for acknowledgement and similarity, on the one hand, and the need for uniqueness and individuation, on the other. The literature on this topic also highlights the cultural dimension of these needs (McAdoo, 1993): more individualistic cultures, such as in the US, value more highly the development of autonomy whereas more collectivist cultures value intimate and family relationships. In collectivist cultures, unlike those that extol individualism, people's need to belong is most prevalent and a high saturation of these needs is associated with wellbeing (Chun & MacDermid, 1997), while emotional autonomy is associated with the presence of problematic behaviours (Fuhrman & Holmbeck, 1995). In any case, the need both for autonomy and for belonging are maintained, in varying proportions, for the purposes of identity construction. In the context of the family, these needs have been empirically translated as the curvilinear idea of functioning with respect to the variable of cohesion (Olson, 1986). Family cohesion, defined as the perception of emotional bonds and loyalty between family members, is represented as being curvilinear. This is to say that optimal functioning is located in the middle: neither excessive emotional bonding (a situation of enmeshment) nor too little (a situation of disengagement). This attempt to hold together aspects of closeness and distance-separation through a median solution is, according to Green and Werner (1996), the result of confusion between cohesion and enmeshment. The former indicates the strength of the bond and the latter the clearness of the boundaries. The two variables are orthogonal and linear. In this way, high differentiation would be typical of families with a strong bond and clear boundaries while, at the opposite end, low differentiation would be typical of families with a weak bond and diffuse boundaries. The interesting debate that has arisen as a result reveals how difficult it is to conceptualize and, even more so, to empirically translate relational constructs and processes that function according to an "and-and" modality. The first solution translates this need by means of a curvilinear model and the second with an orthogonal model. But both models are conceived of in terms of a metaphor of horizontality and spatiality. A satisfactory understanding of the process of differentiation can be obtained, in our opinion, by connecting the horizontal-spatial axis to the vertical-temporal axis. In terms of family studies, we are able to connect in this way the process of adjusting distances to the process of intergenerational transmission. This does not have to do so much or exclusively with keeping to the middle ground, neither too far nor too close, but involves mediating or negotiating in the sense of giving form to what we have received and continue to receive from the significant others in our lives and from our generational history, transforming it into something new. The capacity to establish intimate relationships while maintaining our own boundaries (observational level of family relationships in progress) depends on how the intergenerational passage and negotiation have come about and continue to do so. This task belongs to each family and is mediated by the *meanings and representations* that a specific culture and family and social history carry with respect to the bond. Is it important to express emotional closeness? If so, how? Is it important to be loyal, and how is this manifested? How does one establish intimate bonds that respect the individuality-uniqueness of every family member?

We differentiate ourselves through a process that takes place within and not outside *belonging*. This requires the *acknowledgement* of the other and the bond one has with him or her (capacity for empathy), not the elimination of the other and his or her *misrecognition*. Capturing this process is difficult, but in any case it acts to determine the current state of distinction-differentiation, both on a personal and family level. The result of this process of distinction is the capacity for autonomy, understood as the capacity to answer for oneself as a specific member of a family, as a specific couple, and as a specific family. To "respond" for oneself implies perceiving one's own boundaries, assuming one's own decisions and responsibilities but it also implies responding *to someone*, as the etymology reminds us. The assumption of one's own uniqueness as a person and as a family is an exchange between family members and between generations. And it is in the exercise of this exchange and negotiation that new bonds are generated and old ones are given new meaning.

In this process of distinction, which hinges on acknowledgement, it is also possible to observe affective and ethical aspects. The former have to do with the capacity for cognitive-affective acknowledgement of feelings, thoughts, and attitudes as belonging to oneself and to others (the study of attributive processes is extremely significant for this purpose); the latter have to do with the capacity to acknowledge and assume the family function-role, that is, one's interpersonal and intergenerational legitimization. We conceive of the generational passage in a nondeterministic sense: it is the product of a negotiation in which multiple generations play a role. An individual who has differentiated him- or herself has a margin of freedom and the possibility of taking decisions with respect to a family's inherited legacy, even if not everyone occupies an equal position in terms of family and cultural history. When speaking of intergenerational transmission, one could think in terms of mental space that has already been "occupied" by the preceding generations with respect to those that follow. It is thus possible to have many constraints and little freedom when much has been imposed upon us in a limiting or ambiguous way. On the other hand, one might experience few constraints and many opportunities when much has been given in a clear and unambiguous way in order to promote the new generation. In the first case, the new generation will have little space for itself and low distinctivity (or, in other words, high confusion); in the second case, there will be ample space in which the new generation can work on its inheritance and, therefore, will have a high possibility of distinction. When the process of related distinction functions efficiently, it makes innovative transformation possible. This solution allows people and generations to develop their personal uniqueness while maintaining belonging with the family. Its dangers and failures derive from the impasse or refusal, whether active (counter-dependent) or passive (due to negation and forgetfulness). In this latter category fall all those positions that make of the *new* (a new age of life, as when a young person takes on adult status or when a new couple or family is born) an absolute beginning without roots and therefore without acknowledgement of past family and/or social history. Negotiation teaches us, however, that the end result is produced by more than one generation, even if each bears different responsibilities.

THE INTERGENERATIONAL DIMENSION IN THE FAMILY AND SOCIETY

The relational perspective induces us to see the bond between subjects or, put more precisely, to see and define family members as subjects bound to the history of the generations. A new couple is in fact the meeting point between two family histories: spouses negotiate, often unawares, two life styles learned in their families of origin. The identity of the new family is connected to a balanced exchange with the preceding generations that safeguards the distinctivity of and, at the same time, allows for the acknowledgement of what has been transmitted. Nevertheless, thinking in terms of *generations* has become rare within families: the newborn child is represented as something possessed and produced by the couple rather than as a new generation on the threshold of history, destined to renew the family patrimony and to contribute to society. To conceive of one's child as a new generation confers a strong identity on the family, as was the case in our culture not so long ago. At the opposite extreme, losing a sense of multiple generations means that families have weak identities. Reading family dynamics without a generational perspective reveals the short-sightedness of much psychological reflection. Psychological research has often interpreted family accounts from the point of view of one member of the family—the mother, the child, the adolescent or the young person—without connecting them to the perspective of the other generation and without connecting them to the generational history.

The intergenerational dimension concerns not only the bonds and exchanges between the generations within the family, but also the bond between the family and society. The literature has often kept the relationship between the family and society in the background and has treated it in a generic way. The social realm has been defined as the environment outside the family and parallel modalities have been found in the inner functioning of the family and its way of relating to society (Beavers, 1982; Constantine, 1986; Reiss, 1981). Other authors have taken a sociocultural perspective, seeing the social environment as cultural history to be considered in parallel with family history and genetic influences. McGoldrick et al.'s (1993) model is a good example of this approach:[3] it hypothesizes the existence of an inclusive relationship between a person, family, and cultural context and accentuates the central role played by sociocultural events for individual and family trajectories. At the same time, this model acknowledges the family's function in mediating the exchanges that occur between individuals and the sociocultural context. The relational–intergenerational point of view challenges us to further enrich this perspective and to read the social realm not as a generic context or as a cultural context that surrounds the family but as a social context that has been organized by multiple generations. Thus, the same questions that have to do with the bond between family generations can be extended to the social organism: where does the social dynamic structure the exchange between generations? Does it favour or obstruct reciprocity and productive passages between the generations?

Just as in the family, generative and/or degenerative processes are at work in society: the former produce wellbeing, allow for the development of identity, and enhance family and social histories, whereas the latter produce distress, undermine family history, and cause the deterioration and disappearance of social traditions, and even of civilization itself. The exchanges between family and social worlds are closely connected and whatever takes place between the generations in families influences whatever occurs between the generations in society, and vice versa. This is an aspect that is not infrequently neglected or, at the least, undervalued. The adult generations may not take into consideration the effect their behaviour in the family has on society. On the other hand, society may repress the fact that the generations are an extension of a reality that originates in the family and may not emphasize the connection between social and family generativity. This is what happens today regarding the difficult passage to adulthood. In a relational perspective, it is important to connect the family generations (qualified by ascendancy–descendancy, by roles and by family members' status) with the social generations (qualified by age, status and social roles). In this way, parents and offspring face each other as *family generations* and adults and young people do the same as *social generations*. It is important to understand how the family and society succeed in holding together different generations and to grasp what relationship exists between the exchange between the generations in a family and the exchange between the generations in society. The relational–intergenerational perspective also represents our point of view in interpreting transitions. In fact, the theme of transition is crucial to our perspective.

THE TRANSITION TO ADULTHOOD

The relationships between family members and, in particular, the exchanges between generations, reveal themselves most emphatically during times of passage, when the family is called on to change its organization and to disclose its strengths and weaknesses. In recent years the theme of transitions has become a leitmotif in the psychological literature (Bengston & Allen, 1993; Ruble & Seidman, 1996; Wapner & Craig-Bray, 1992) thanks, in part, to the theory of family stress and coping. This theory has shifted attention from the analysis of single stages of the family life cycle to the moment of passage from one stage to another and to the coping processes that allow families to face the change (Falicov, 1988). Transitions are prompted by critical events that may be either predictable or unpredictable. The critical aspect of the event resides in the fact that it opens a window on uncertainty, calls for a change and throws up new objectives that may either promote development or constitute an obstacle and a blockage for the family. We might mention among the expected events those resulting from the acquisition of new family members (due to marriages, births and adoptions) and those resulting from losses (deaths, separations, and illnesses). Other equally specific events appear less focused and delimited, such as the transition to adulthood or old age. A crisis set off by a transition offers a privileged opportunity to understand whether the exchange between generations has occurred in the spirit of trust and equality and also whether and to what degree it is possible to modify the relationships within the family in the light of the changes required by the transition. Precisely because transitions reveal and simultaneously test the family's relational interplay, they need to be understood, as Lewin reminds us, as a group intergenerational passage, that is, something that involves the whole organization and affects the relationship between the generations and the family's identity. Each transition is not an automatic passage from one position to another. The transition tests the family, which may, as a result, achieve new objectives; or it might fail, create difficulties in some of its members, cause the family's break-up, etc.

Each transition "is" thus a task. Therefore, the concept of a developmental task (Havighurst, 1972; Newman & Newman, 1995) is understood here in the sense of being relational/intergenerational: the behaviours and attitudes of different family members and different generations have reciprocal effects on the achievement of the transitional task. We shall see this more clearly in the transition to adulthood.

The transitions and passages that a family undertakes in the course of a lifetime present specific characteristics in our society. While in archaic societies most transitions took place by discrete "leaps" and were accompanied by veritable "rites of passage", in modern contemporary society transitions are represented more and more as being individual, relatively undefined (with respect to both modalities and timing), negotiable, little ritualized and with ample margins of choice. An automatic passage has been thus transformed into a transitional path with its own timing. Indeed, as far as timing is concerned, we are witnessing today a temporal dilation of developmental and family passages. This is particularly true in the case of the transition to adulthood of the younger generation.

The extension of the stage of life spanning the transition from childhood to adulthood is an increasingly common phenomenon in industrialized countries (Arnett, 2000; Cavalli & Galland, 1993; Graber & Dubas, 1996;

Palmonari, 1997). As Arnett (2000, 2004) points out, sweeping demographic shifts have taken place over the past half century that have made the late teens and early twenties not simply a brief period of transition to adult roles but a distinct period of the life course, characterized by change and exploration of possible life directions. The transition to adulthood is no longer a short span of time made up of precise steps, but a long transition marked by numerous microtransitions (Breunlin, 1988) beginning in late adolescence. On closer scrutiny, the transition to adult life takes the form of a double transition, from the adolescent phase to that of the young adult and from this to the phase of full adulthood. These are not two well-defined transitions, however: rather, the first has the attributes of a preparatory phase (microtransition), characterized by events such as, for example, acquiring some responsibility in organizations in the social context, only to be followed by the true transition that the young person will accomplish in the next phase (macrotransition), characterized by events such as starting a family or acquiring the status of a worker with significant responsibilities. In the preparatory phase, the foundations are laid and the conditions created that will either promote or hinder the passage to adulthood (Scabini & Cigoli, 2000). This process is thus characterized by gradualism and sees the young person move from a position of total "social marginality" (Lewin, 1951), intrinsic to adolescence, to a position of partial marginality in the phase of young adulthood, to finally reach a fully acknowledged social position in the adult phase. Today's adolescents are experiencing a condition marked by "status inconsistency" (Hurrelmann, 1989), a condition that is slowly redefined with the passage of time from early adolescence to young adulthood. This expression admirably conveys the situation facing adolescents: a reality characterized by simultaneous divergent demands coming from the different life spheres to which they belong (family, school, peer group, etc.) and in each of which they enjoy varying degrees of inclusion and autonomy. In none of these contexts do adolescents attain to an adult level of responsibility, however, and they are sometimes unable to count on anyone to carry out the function of coordinating the array of demands.

Moreover, the ordering of traditional markers of this transition has now been altered by a modern life style that increasingly allows previously made choices to be revised and reversed (Carrà & Marta, 1995). Young adults often explore a variety of possible life directions in love, work and world views. Young adulthood is a time of life when many different directions remain open, when little about the future has been decided for certain, when the scope of independent exploration of life's possibilities is greater for most people than it will be at any other time of life.

The term "young adult" highlights the salient aspects of this period of life in which the young person embodies the contradiction of being an adult, at least potentially, but at the same time is a growing, changing person on the way to forming an adult identity. Thus, we use the term "young adult" to indicate neither a chronological expansion of adolescence nor the first phase of adulthood but, rather, a time of life that is unique in being a bridge or a passage between two conditions, adolescence and adulthood, and that covers a span of time that extends from 19 to 28–30 years of age. In this sense, the construct can be differentiated from the one Arnett identified as "emerging adulthood", which indicates instead a chronological phase ranging from 18 to 25 years of age.

The demographic characteristics of the transition

The protraction of the transition to adult status has been noted in recent years by numerous authors, demonstrating that it is a widespread phenomenon but with very different characteristics depending on one's country of origin (Rossi, 1997). Iacovou and Berthoud (2001), in an analysis of data gathered by the European Community Household Panel, have identified two behavioural models in young adults. In the first model, which groups together the nations of southern Europe (Italy, Spain, Portugal, and Greece) together with Austria and Ireland, individuals leave the parental home either when they marry or when they become parents. In the second model, the northern European model (Germany, Denmark, Scandinavia, Holland, UK, France, Belgium, and Luxembourg), individuals leave the parental home much earlier and move through multiple intermediate stages such as living alone, living with a partner and a long period of marriage without children. An initial examination of these data allows us to ascertain that the disparities found between the two groups of nations with respect to young adults remaining in the parental home are not merely the reflection of longer school attendance or differing unemployment levels in the two geographical areas. In fact, even when we account for educational achievement and the labour market, the disparities between the two groupings remain practically unchanged (Vogel, 2002). Iacovou's analysis of the data reveals that the differences between north and south are concentrated within a relatively short time span. At 17 years of age, the differences are essentially nonexistent: the overwhelming majority of young people live with their parents, are single, and childless. Significant differences begin to appear around 20 years of age and diminish again at around the age of 30. At 23 years of age, 72% of northern European women have moved away from their families of origin, as opposed to 27% of their counterparts in southern Europe. The same trend is seen in young men: 47% from northern Europe have left home compared to only 15% of their peers in southern Europe (Figure 1.2).

In other words, in terms of their relations with their families of origin, marked differences among young Europeans appear between the ages of 20 and 30 years. The phases preceding and following this period do not reveal significant differences in this population. In particular, the proportion of men from southern Europe between 25 and 29 years who are unmarried

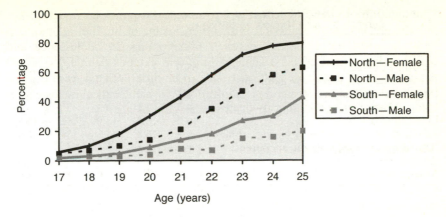

Figure 1.2 Proportion of men and women who have left home or formed a partnership, by age (adapted from Iacovou & Berthoud, 2001).

and childless is 30 percentage points higher than northern males (73.7% versus 45.25%). The number of women 25 to 29 years old living in the south of Europe who are still single and childless is twice that in the north (49.95% versus 23.4%).

In the US, most young adults leave home by age 18 or 19 and many are living in semi-autonomous situations such as dorms, remaining financially dependent on their parents (Schoeni & Ross, 2005; Settersten, Furstenberg, & Rumbaut, 2005). One-third of emerging adults go off to college after high school and spend the next several years in some combination of independent living. Only about 40% of men and 30% of women remain at home until marriage (Arnett, 2000; Goldscheider, 1997). Thus, young adults in the US are also remaining dependent on their parents for material and housing support later into the life course (Toguchi Swartz, 2005).

As this brief overview shows, the transition to adulthood in Europe takes place in cultural contexts that differ greatly and offer diverse challenges and resources. The transition to adulthood is progressively breaking down into a sequence of individual transitory stages based on a range of social and temporal models (Hurrelmann, 1989; Hurrelmann & Engel, 1989). However, the timing, duration and order of these passages vary considerably among individuals and cultures (Kerckhoff & Macrae, 1993; Miller & Heaton, 1991; Sherrod, Haggerty, & Featherman, 1993).

THE SPECIFICITY OF THE MEDITERRANEAN MODEL AND THE NEW ROLE OF THE FAMILY OF ORIGIN

As Hurrelmann (1989) has pointed out, the Italian situation is the most emblematic of the Mediterranean group of nations, offering a glimpse of

Table 1.2 Reasons cited by young people for continuing to live with parents, by age (Multiscopo Survey)

	18–19	20–24	25–29	30-3-4	Total
I'm still studying	58.9	31.1	16.1	5.0	27.5
I'm fine this way, I have my autonomy	41.4	46.6	50.8	54.4	48.1
I don't feel like leaving	3.1	6.2	8.1	9.5	6.7
I should have to give up too many things	4.3	5.1	4.3	5.5	4.8
I can't find a job	10.4	18.5	18.0	16.2	16.8
I can't go to the expense of having a house	9.2	16.8	18.8	18.3	16.4
It would be disagreeable for my parents	8.2	7.5	6.6	5.9	7.1
Parents need me	1.4	2.6	3.5	7.4	3.3
Other	1.9	3.4	5.0	5.9	4.0

things to come in the other countries of southern Europe, and partly in the north as well. Bearing this in mind, let us now delineate a framework for the transition to adulthood in Italy. The data from the latest cycle of the Multiscopo Survey reveal a snapshot of Italy in 1998. At that time, 95% of children between 18 and 19 years of age lived in the parental home, as compared to 88.3% of 20- to 24-year-olds and 59.3% of 25- to 29-year-olds; 21.8% of 30- to 34-year-olds continued to live with their parents. The principal reason cited by young people for continuing to live with their parents is that they experience a sense of well-being within the family. This situation turns out to be the norm (Table 1.2).

It is interesting to note that young people in the age groups 18- to 19-year-olds and 20- to 24-year-olds cite a higher percentage of objective obstacles as reasons for remaining in their parents' home ("I'm still studying", "I can't find a job"), while for the following two age groups the motives are primarily subjective ("I'm fine this way", "I don't feel like leaving" . . .). It is thus possible to distinguish between two distinct moments in the transition. At first, the young adult judges his/her situation to be "normal" because there are well-founded reasons for continuing to live at home: finishing one's studies, the absence of work, the shortage of flats. Then, with the passing of time, the attitude changes, probably because objective motivations no longer constitute real obstacles and the young person convinces him- or herself that it's not so bad living at home after all (Caprara, Scabini, & Sgritta, 2003; Sgritta, 2002). In analysing the American situation, Arnett points out that the striking characteristic of emerging adulthood is its remarkable demographic variability, reflecting the wide scope of individual volition during these years. Emerging adulthood is the only time in life in which nothing is normative demographically. The demographic variability and unpredictability of emerging adulthood is a reflection of the experimental and exploratory quality of the period (Arnett, 2002). Arnett (2000) describes this situation, emphasizing the role of individual factors or motivations, such as accepting responsibility for oneself, taking decisions in an independent manner, acquiring economic independence that, taken alone, do not appear to be relevant for understanding and interpreting the situation of young Italians.

We can only understand the condition of young people in Italy, and in the south of Europe more generally, from a relational perspective that takes into account the reciprocal modality of the parent–child relationship and the changes that have occurred in recent decades. Until a few decades ago the usually conflictive nature of the relations between parents and their young adult children clearly indicated that the latter were seeking their own future, one that would be different and independent from the future their parents desired for them. This was to be a future fundamentally *outside* the family because it began when the children left the parental home to become adults. Today, the atmosphere in families is undoubtedly less conflictive, to the extent that the transition to adulthood takes place, at least in part, within the family of origin. The path young Italians take towards the achievement of autonomy from their families is not characterized by a series of trials and attempts at distancing themselves from the parental home until the right moment to leave arrives, once and for all. Rather, it is a slow and progressive restructuring of the relationship with parents based on a belief in the necessity of prolonging cohabitation due to objective, external difficulties (the difficulty of finding a first job or of keeping a job) as well as on the reciprocal psychological advantage for all concerned, as we shall see.

It is interesting to note that some studies in the US (see, for example, Settersten et al., 2005) have also found that American young adults say that they have a relationship with their parents that is not at all conflictive and that they live with their parents as young adults because they need to finish school, land a job or save for housing (Toguchi Swartz, 2005).

The uniqueness of the Italian situation is determined by the fact that almost all Italian young adults share housing with their parents until the time when they start their own families, thus generating the phenomenon of the presence under one roof of two adult generations (sometimes also three, if a member of the first generation—a grandparent of the young person— for varying reasons lives in the same home).

The slowing down of the transition to adulthood has endowed the family of origin with more value and more influence during a period of the life cycle during which, in past decades, it has tended to play only a minor role. The family, with its crucial position at the intersecting point of gender and generational lines, has always fulfilled the function of sustenance and support for its offspring, but this willingness of families to support their younger members in the long transition to adulthood is a new phenomenon. As a matter of fact, the slowing down of this transition is possible only because young adults can count on their families. Thus, the transition to adulthood occurs within the family of origin: indeed, it depends on the family of origin, or, rather, on the quality of family relationships, for its successful outcome (Scabini, 1995, 2000a; Sroufe, 1991; Youniss & Smollar,

1985). Research carried out on the family's function during the transition to adult status demonstrates that its role in providing support cuts across different models of the transition. The family constitutes an important resource in facing this transition, whether young people reside with their families of origin or whether they have tried to live on their own (Amato, 1994; Holahan, Valentiner, & Moos, 1994; Van Wel, Linssen, & Abma, 2000). Furthermore, the family of origin is more important today than ever because significant adults outside the family have practically disappeared (Lanz, Rosnati, Iafrate, & Marta, 1999; Tonolo, 1999). In other words, today's young people, far from waging an intergenerational battle within the family, seem to have given up the search outside the family for adults who can provide alternative points of reference to those offered by their parents. Their lives appear to oscillate between two groups: first, the family, which is becoming ever more peer-oriented and, second, but to a lesser extent, their circle of peers. Other adult reference points are not considered to be significant. The protraction of the transition to adulthood requires young people to assume new characteristics due to the fact that the passage from adolescence to adulthood has been replaced by a series of micro-transitions that lead from adolescence (beginning earlier than in the past) to young adulthood and from this to full adult status. Late adolescence and young adulthood become crucial developmental phases because these are times when individuals are called on to make many choices and to engage in a variety of behaviours that have the potential to influence the rest of their lives.

OFFSPRING'S AND PARENTAL TASKS DURING THE TRANSITION TO ADULTHOOD: A JOINT ENTERPRISE

The primary aim of the transition consists in allowing the young person to reach adulthood.[4] In real terms, this translates into emancipation from the parental home. In other words, it requires the devising and realization in a short time of a life plan. This will set the stage for the acquisition of economic independence and social responsibility—by means of entry into the work force and civil society—as well as for the shouldering of family responsibilities—through the choice of a stable, affective relationship, and the "blueprint" of a plan to build a new family. The achievement of this goal is a "joint developmental enterprise" shared by parents and offspring (Cigoli, 1997; Noack, Kerr, & Olah, 1999; Scabini, 1995; Sroufe, 1991). This task should thus be seen in relational terms. Parents also have a specific, dual role to play: on the one hand, they must promote this plan and legitimize their offspring as they undertake new tasks; on the other hand, they are required to undergo a generative transformation themselves. The key process that allows for the successful completion of the transition is one of correlated distinction that involves both parents and offspring.

During this transition the family must synchronize two antagonistic forces: the need to maintain family unity and a sense of belonging (felt most keenly by parents) and the push towards separation and autonomy (felt most strongly by offspring). The positive outcome of this process, that is, the acquisition by children of a "distinct" position that enables aspects of uniqueness as well as of interdependence to emerge, seems to be linked to forces that see both parents and offspring in the role of protagonists. Stierlin has emphasized that parents' attitudes about letting their children go act as modelling forces that can either positively or negatively influence boundaries having to do with separation. These attitudes are rooted in a family history that, particularly during this phase, reveals its progressive or regressive tendencies. Stierlin (1974, 1975) identified three attitudes that parents may have regarding the approaching separation of their offspring: neither the denial nor underestimation of the event, at one extreme, nor an enthusiastic welcoming at the other extreme, seem to constitute useful and effective inducements for children to become independent.

The most satisfactory attitude is found in parents who express sadness over their child's separation but at the same time are convinced that they will be able to overcome the inevitable emptiness that this separation entails for them. The theme of loss is particularly prominent during this transition, even if it is mitigated by the long duration of the process. While all that the family must leave behind becomes increasingly evident with time, the new life that is to come remains shadowy. Full adulthood, especially in terms of plans for a new family, has many uncertain and unstable aspects today. Only in the long term will parents see evidence of a commitment to carry on the generational history. The right distance is thus connected to the process of transmission and acquisition of the biological, affective, and ethical inheritance. The young person must find his or her place in the family genealogy and accept an active role in carrying on the family project. Parents, on the other hand, must promote a gradual handover of adult roles while maintaining a supportive position from a distance.

The successful completion of this transition that sees the young generation taking on full adult responsibility also depends on how well parents have been able to responsibly care for their children as adolescents: this means adopting an attitude of "flexible protection" (Scabini, 1995) and fulfilling a function of personalized guidance. Flexible protection is an attitude that takes into account both the aspects of dependency that continue during adolescence as well as aspects of autonomy. The exercise of personalized guidance consists in finding strategies that help adolescents make their own choices and in supporting them in realizing these choices. The acquisition of adult identity is promoted when adolescents are able to count on families that make space for dialogue (where family members can encounter, as well as confront, each other and where there is negotiation between different points of view) and provide direction to the young person (thus transmitting values, monitoring, and providing guidance in choice

making). "Flexible protection" is a key term not only for the family's
internal relations but also with regard to the function of mediation with
society that the family is increasingly required to carry out, often in new
and, above all, flexible forms. The boundary between the family and the
social realm is mobile, needing to be negotiated over and over again all the
while avoiding strategies that may produce a schism between individual,
family and social spheres. In terms of the parent–child relationship during
the phase of young adulthood, flexible protection also implies a gradual
weakening of protective aspects and the strengthening of emancipatory
aspects that promote the acceptance of responsibility. In the young adult's
"ongoing family", this gradual push towards freedom may wane because
parents and offspring are able to fulfil reciprocal needs through the family,
thus producing a dangerous stability. This gives rise to sort of intergenerational stalemate that hinders separation. Scabini and Cigoli (2000) have
called this phenomenon "reciprocal relational advantage" to emphasize the
active role that both generations play in protracting the transition.

OFFSPRING AND PARENTS IN THE TRANSITION: RECIPROCAL ADVANTAGE

How do the dovetailing needs of parents and children during this period
manifest themselves? On the one hand, young adults stake out a "free
zone" within the family home that is completely autonomous and private
and in which they enjoy considerable freedom. As our research has shown
(Scabini, 2000a), they may thus count on the support and resources of their
family of origin without any particular constraints. Faced with an uncertain
future, adolescents and young adults see their families as their fundamental
source of security. As Mortimer and Larson (2002) point out, our complex
technological society calls on young people to acquire ever more specialized
abilities and skills on various levels. The family represents the context in
which they can prolong the time of preparation for entering a social arena
that is increasingly competitive. Based in this supportive family context,
young people can gradually venture out into society to gain "controlled"
experience in the working world, which constitutes their major worry. In
the same way, they can approach experience in the affective realm, putting
off to some future time the decision to start a family. Thus, the young
person is able to enjoy a lengthy moratorium in which to test him- or
herself in the world of work and the affections without being obliged to
fully accept the limitations and responsibilities that these choices imply. For
their part, parents are content with the aspect of relational truce that
characterizes this phase, finding that they benefit indirectly. As a result,
they can prolong their parental function without, however, having to suffer
the difficulties typical of the period of offspring's adolescence. Interviews
with parents clearly reveal that they easily identify with their children

inasmuch as the younger generation enjoys a lifestyle both free and rich with possibilities, a lifestyle that the older generation could not have experienced in their own youth but desired nonetheless. Moreover, these parents, in behaving according to the modality of comprehensive dialogue, achieve an ideal in the parent–child relationship that was not available to them in their own families of origin. Parents and children also *share representations* regarding their future. They are in agreement in seeing adult life in a negative light, marked by uncertainty and precariousness in the social realm—the difficulty of achieving one's working aspirations—as well as in the family realm—the difficulty of finding a reliable partner. The most important area of personal investment is above all the professional context in which the young person is required to face the challenge in a way that is in keeping with his or her level of aspiration. Parents and offspring hold in common an idea of *adult identity* and *self-fulfilment* in which aspects dominate that are self-centred in nature and fundamentally unconnected to, and cut off from, the generative dimension, with its concomitant responsibilities towards a future family. Work and love are understood above all to be opportunities to express oneself and much less as contexts in which to accept responsibilities and commit to bonds. Once again, affective aspects have the upper hand over latent ethical aspects.

The long transition to adulthood within the family of origin is thus the result of parents' and offspring's joined forces: both gain from it a psychic and relational advantage. This "solution", which prolongs the transition, may be a functional answer to a variety of social problems and to increasingly complex requirements that society is imposing on young people. It could also represent a danger to the development of identity if it becomes a condition of *intergenerational stalemate*. If they are to prevent such a stalemate, both offspring and parents must undertake to change their perspective regarding generativity. Offspring are required to make a challenging leap forwards in position and include in their concept of self-fulfilment the care for and responsibility towards new lives. Parents, for their part, must redirect towards new goals and objectives the commitment to generativity that they have hitherto dedicated to nurturing family relationships.

PARENTAL GENERATIVITY AND SOCIAL GENERATIVITY

As Snarey (1993) observed, parents are called on to undertake a specific transition, and that is, to move "from *parental generativity* to *social generativity*, thus augmenting their own culture's symbolic system and passing it on to successive generations" (Kotre, 1984, p. 14). In this way, while parents enact parental generativity with respect to their own children, social generativity implies that they are committed not only to raising their own offspring but also, on a larger scale, to actively contributing to the

realization of the generation to which their children belong. Social generativity is aimed at the future of all young people who are on the threshold
of adulthood: it promotes an ethical cycle of generational inclusion and
supports the establishment of *intergenerational fairness.*[5] This movement
away from purely parental generativity to social generativity is particularly
critical today in a cultural climate that is decidedly individualistic and that
permeates both the parent–child relationship and the relations between the
generations of adults and youth in society at large.

McAdams and de St Aubin (1998) have pointed out that a sign of
generativity's failure coincides with excessive self-interest. Even parents'
attitude towards their offspring may draw on the logic of self-interest if, as
often happens today, the parents are tempted to see mirror images of
themselves in the few children they produce, considering them to be "their"
children and not new family and social generations. Parental generativity
can thus acquire strong protective tendencies and weak emancipatory
elements. Nevertheless, we must remind ourselves that this attitude cannot
be understood in isolation from the realities of the social context. Society
presents us with a dynamic between the adult and young generations that is
decidedly unfavourable to the latter: this condition has been justly labelled
as *generational unfairness* (Donati, 1991). This is the case in some countries
in the south of Europe, such as Spain (Cordon, 1997) and Italy, in which
the Welfare State has greatly supported the active generation, now adult or
elderly, in past decades and is no longer able to do the same for the younger
generation who is about to enter the status of adulthood. The younger
generations must make a difficult entry into an environment that is both
competitive and greedy in the way it is dividing up resources that are
securely in the hands of the adult and elderly generations. It is as if adults,
in the social context, have acted in ways that neglect their role as parents:
they have lost sight of the generative quality of investment in future
generations. Thus, the generations appear solidly united within the family
and solidly opposed to each other and competitive in society. The dynamic
underlying the intergenerational exchange between family and society is
therefore founded on processes of division and compensation rather than
on those of transformation. Parents, by prolonging the protective aspects of
family life, compensate for the injustice present in society that they uncon-
sciously contribute to.

CONCLUDING REFLECTIONS

The family is a specific organization of primary relationships that holds
together and interrelates the primary human differences: those of gender
(male and female), generations (parents and offspring) and lineage (the
maternal and paternal family trees). It also creates a relational product,
offspring—that is to say, a new generation.

In this chapter we have presented our perspective, which, from now in this work, will be referred to as relational–intergenerational. We have presented our interpretative overview of the transition to adulthood in the light of a relational–intergenerational perspective of family and societal dynamics. We have seen that in Western societies, particularly in southern Europe, the younger generation's transition to adulthood is fraught with difficulties. We have seen that aspects related to the sense of belonging have the upper hand in families and are sought out and even tenaciously nurtured by both generations. However, that which appears to be a means of strengthening bonds turns out also to constitute a constraint and a burden when it comes to giving the relationship new form and vitality. Young adults are stifled in their filial identities and adults in their identities as parents: the dimension of planning for the future remains, for both generations, in the background. Young people find it difficult to make the generational leap; adults find it difficult to exercise responsible social generativity. It easy to move from a developmental slow-down to the blockage of identity. The result is that the needs of distinctivity are scarcely taken into consideration at an intergenerational level: the generations turn out to be confused, in the sense of being undifferentiated, in families and opposed in society. In the light of this overview, it is evident that the critical element of the transition is not to be found exclusively or primarily in the fact of parents' and offspring's prolonged cohabitation or excessive closeness, but in the processes that govern this intricate role play between social generations (adults/youth) and family generations (parents/offspring). To safeguard the younger generation's progress towards adulthood, the role played by the adult generation, not only in the family but also in society, is crucial: it must transform its generative energies by more explicitly directing them towards the social context. Only by opposing the dangerous schism between the family and social realms can a constructive generational "change of guard" take place, accompanied by the strengthening of the younger generation in its task of embracing adult responsibilities.

2 "Family research" versus "family-related research": a crucial difference

INTRODUCTION

Defining one's object of study is a crucial phase in research methodology. If a researcher does not have clear ideas about what he or she is studying, it becomes extremely difficult to design a research project that is consistent in all its parts. Research on family relations inevitably runs up against the lack of an explicit definition of the object to be investigated, with the result that studies differ greatly from each other and there is inconsistency between the use of research strategies and techniques for data analysis. What do we mean by "family"? Each one of us is able to answer this question but if we compare our responses we realize that they differ greatly from each other. The definition of the object of study cannot be independent of the theoretical framework that guides and directs the research process. According to the relational–intergenerational perspective that was described in Chapter 1, the family is an organization of primary relations founded on the differences of gender, generation, and family lineage. The family, in this perspective, is analysed both on an interactive level, that is, in the present by looking at the "action taking place between participants", and on a relational level, that is, by seeking to apprehend the bond that precedes the interaction in progress and constitutes its meaningful context. Interaction is imbued with meaning when we are able to discern underlying relationships. Approaching family studies from a specific perspective implies giving attentive consideration to research methodology, to the way in which research able to capture the organization of relationships should be structured. Theory (the point of view adopted with respect to the family) and method (how it is studied) are intrinsically connected: in other words, as Campbell maintained in the 1970s (Campbell, 1970), method and object come into being together. What we know and how we know it are inextricably linked. The goal of tightening the connection between theory research and applications was put forward by David Olson in the mid-1970s (Olson, 1976) after the sharp separation between these fields was noted. The same author (Larsen & Olson, 1990) returned to this preoccupation at the methodological level, underlining the need to maintain consistency between various component parts of a

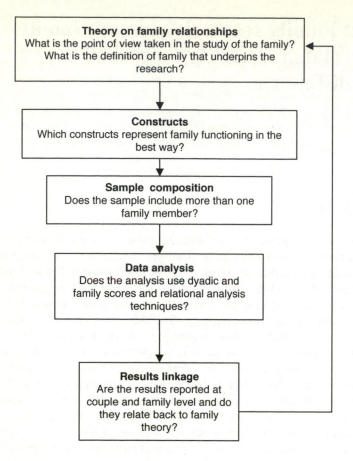

Figure 2.1 Crucial phases of the research cycle in family studies (adapted from Larsen & Olson, 1990).

study. Consistency between the different research phases is an aspect of the research's validity that becomes especially crucial in family studies (Figure 2.1).

A crucial phase in every research process is the formulation of a clear statement of the theoretical perspective: theory determines the questions asked, which determine the method used, which determines the data analysis performed, which in turn leads back to the theory used. Method is the way towards the object of study. In family studies the theoretical perspective is not always explicitly stated, thus making it difficult to maintain consistency between the different phases. We know that the family-object, understood to be a relational organization, is a surplus, that is, a totality-unit that is more than the sum of its parts. It is a multiple, complex unity that can never be fully captured. A vision such as ours that gives centre stage to relational complexity cannot be translated into a relativistic (one point of view is as good as the next) yet approximate research philosophy. It is necessary to design research strategies that are able to approach the object as completely and closely as possible. Bray, Maxwell, and Cole (1995) maintain that the study of the family is intrinsically complicated due to the complex nature of the relationships within it. Studying families involves the consideration of a relational object. This assumption is central to methodology because it means that researchers have to choose appropriate methods to study relationships and, in particular, relationships in the family.

The study of family relations will mainly revolve around dyadic or family constructs, that is, constructs that refer to a subsystem of the family organization, such as the mother–child dyad (for example, mother–child communication), or that refer to the family as a whole. In the past 10 years, some authors have pointed to the difficulty in using family constructs. Indeed, asking respondents to think about "the family" or "our family" is an abstraction that may create error in the assessment of family functioning due to differences in meaning. Martin and Cole (1993) suggested that the best way to tackle the issues of meaning in family instruments is to clarify who is speaking and who is being described. It seems clear that not all members of a family interact in the same way with each other, and these differences in interactive processes may represent important information to obtain. It may be more fruitful to ask about dyadic relationships among family members than to ask individuals to generalize to the abstract concept of "the family" (Cole & Jordan, 1989). The choice of the type of construct to use should not be confused with the choice of unit of measurement and unit of analysis. The unit of measurement is determined by the subjects from whom data are gathered. It thus depends directly on the type of instrument employed in the research. If this is a self-report instrument, the unit of measurement is the single individual who provides the responses. The unit of analysis refers to the level to which the researcher wishes to generalize the data, and to the way these data are used. The choice of unit of analysis constitutes the crucial phase of family research. It is in this phase that one encounters the most common research inconsistencies, for example studying the mother–child relationship while taking into consideration only the child's perceptions or considering both the mother's as well as the child's perceptions but analysing them without taking cognizance of the fact that these perceptions are dependent on each other.

THE CHOICE OF THE UNIT OF ANALYSIS

Debates about the unit of analysis typically focus on methodological problems, neglecting the importance of the theoretical framework. The discussions about the unit of analysis in family research have been ongoing (e.g.

Carlson, 1989; Grotevant, 1989; Larsen & Olson, 1990) and usually revolve around the issues of perspective (insider, outsider, or multiple perspectives) and data analysis procedures used to maintain the unit of analysis in the original study design. In 1964 Straus wrote, "a discipline concerned with groups cannot depend on measurement of the characteristics of individuals . . . it is necessary to move to the next level of abstraction and develop ways of measuring group properties" (Straus, 1964, p. 9). Even after 40 years this statement is still valid! Thus, we need to develop methods that respect the group specificity, thinking of groups as "something different than the sum of persons" (Lewin, 1948). What, then, is the most suitable unit of analysis for family research? Fortunately or unfortunately, there are no right or wrong answers. The only support for the decisions made in research is the theoretical conceptualization used. For this reason, we can assert that theory lays the foundation for the choice of unit of analysis. Studies on the family are based on different units of analysis and types of data. Some research collects data from only one family member, who describes his/her family. Strictly speaking, statements derived from this type of data reflect only the particular view of that family member. As Feetham (1988) proposes, this type of research can be considered family-related study. In relational-level data collection, researchers obtain data from two or more family members; however, when one collects information about interactions from multiple family members' perspectives, the amount of information increases and data analysis becomes more complex. In this case, researchers have to choose particular techniques of analysis, whether data are based on the dyad or the group, or else obtain a single new score representing some characteristics of the family unit. This second type of research can be defined as family research. In keeping with our approach, the research we have conducted on family relationships has essentially focused on dyadic and family constructs (parent–child communication, parent–child support, cohesion) and has used the family triad (mother, father, child) or tetrad as the units of analysis. Moreover, this research has attempted to highlight the differences between genders and generations (parent–child) and to compare their respective points of view on relationships. In *family research* it is important to collect information both on what is shared between family members (what they have in common and that derives from their history together) and individual perspectives (what family members are characterized by). In reviewing techniques to deal with data from multiple family members, Deal (1995) proposed a distinction between a convergent perspective and a divergent perspective. The convergent perspective asserts that the reality of the family lies in what its members hold in common, while the divergent perspective affirms that the reality of the family may be found in the disparate, or non-overlapping, reports of its members. If the former perspective is taken, then self-reports are sources of shared experience representing interpersonal processes in the family. If the divergent perspective is taken, then individual self-reports reflect each source's unique experiences and attitudes and not the interpersonal processes of the family system. One way we have accessed the multiple levels present in the family is to compare and integrate the approaches of convergence and divergence in order to safeguard both shared and individual aspects. The family is whatever its members hold in common in terms of a shared past and a jointly created present but, at the same time, each family member has his or her own point of view. In true family research, it is necessary to gather information about what family members share—what they have in common, the product of their combined history—but also about each person's individual perspective. Once the unit of analysis has been chosen (which must be at least dyadic, in our opinion) it is necessary to specify on which analytical level the data are to be analysed. As a matter of fact, the study of families touches on several levels of analysis: individual, dyadic and group. This consideration has directed family researchers' efforts towards an adjustment of methodologies in accordance with these theoretical assumptions.

FAMILY SCORES: FROM THE UNIT TO THE DYAD, FROM THE DYAD TO THE FAMILY

An important concern in family research has to do with how to assess families as units in contrast to collecting only individual perceptions. Indeed, much research on family relationships considers only the individual point of view. This approach allows the researcher to obtain only individual perceptions of the family and not relational data. Fisher, Kokes, Ransom, Philips, and Rudd (1985) and Larsen and Olson (1990) think that data obtained in this way are not true family data because they are individual perceptions. It is not enough to collect data from multiple family members and to consider this as family research: tt is necessary to choose specific techniques coherent with the relational nature of this type of data. Two main approaches are used by researchers to study family relationships with quantitative data. The first is to create second-order variables that aggregate information belonging to different members. The second is to carry out a statistical analysis that is able to account for the non-independence of the data and that makes it possible to compare different points of view.

Second-order data

Some analytical procedures act on data across the dyadic/family unit of analysis, but this type of analysis is not second-order data. For example, if in a sample composed of husbands and wives the correlation index is calculated, this index could not be considered a dyadic score but only an individual score because it is an individual unit of analysis. Indeed, in this case, the correlation index reflects the similarity between the men's group and the women's group and not the similarity within the marital dyad. Second-order data are a synthetic measure that accounts for the complexity of the dyad/family without losing information at the individual level. Although there are different ways to obtain synthetic scores to assess dyadic and/or family aspects, it is difficult to decide when to use second-order data and which type of second-order data are more suitable to the research's aims and best safeguard its consistency. We will now look at the principal scores used in our family research.

Arithmetic mean

This is derived from the sum of the scores from the two members in the dyad, divided by two:

$$M = \frac{X_{mt} + X_{ch}}{2}$$

Where X_{mt} is the mother's score and X_{ch} is the child's score. This reflects the arithmetic centre of the distribution of family members' scores: for instance, in the case of dyadic scores it provides a representation of the dyad as a unit and allows us to compare different dyads. When using this score, one must keep in mind that it does not take into account the differences between or among the contributing scores. Indeed, if the difference among family members' scores is small, the arithmetic mean provides an accurate report of the real dyadic/family situation and of the position of the dyad/family on the scale. But if the difference is significant, this type of dyadic score is not representative of the dyadic score.[6] In our research, the arithmetic mean was used to create a synthetic index of the adolescent's perceptions of relationships with father and with mother as a way to obtain an indicator of the parental relationship. To explore the connection between a child's future orientation and relational factors (the quality of family relations—measured through relational support) as well as individual factors (self-esteem and perception of the social world, as measured through the sense of coherence), a parental support score was devised based on the average between the child's perception of mother's support and child's perception of father's support (Lanz & Rosnati, 2002).

Discrepancy score

The discrepancy score is derived from the sum, as an absolute value, of the differences between the responses provided by subject A and those provided by subject B to each item. This sum is then divided by the number of items that make up the scale.

$$D = \frac{\sum_{i=1}^{n} |X_{mti} - X_{chi}|}{n}$$

Where X_{mti} is the mother's score on item i, X_{chi} is the child's score on item i, and n is the number of items. The discrepancy score is used to point out the difference between two family members in a specific dimension. This score provides a measure of the degree of difference or disagreement within the dyad. There are some methodological problems with these scores. First, the discrepancy score's range is influenced both by the variability of responses and by the response categories.[7] To overcome the problem connected to the response categories, we divided the discrepancy score by the maximum discrepancy value provided for the response scale, thus obtaining an invariant indicator for the response categories. Discrepancy scores can also be interpreted as disagreement/agreement scores. As such, they are particularly useful for analysing the differences between generations or between father and mother. In our research, we have used discrepancy scores both for describing perceptual divergences within the family and for analysing the role such divergences play in predicting outcomes. In a study carried out on 295 family triads, with a view to comparing discrepancies on different constructs and to test for any changes linked to the age of the children, discrepancies were calculated between parents and children with respect to perceptions of autonomy in decision making and mutual support in the parent–child relationship (Scabini, 2000a). The discrepancy indices with respect to outcomes were used for the purpose of checking whether the discrepancies between parents and offspring as to perceptions of communication and support were significant predictors of psychosocial risk for late adolescents. A second methodological problem stems from the fact that the difference in scores does not reflect score level.[8] One solution to this dilemma was proposed by Fisher et al. (1985): it involves creating a contingency table that accommodates both level and discrepancy (Table 2.1). This tactic is useful for the purpose of partitioning dyads into convenient types for further analysis.

Unfortunately, there are two related drawbacks to this approach, as pointed out by the authors. First, in the technical sense, important information can be lost when continuous data are reduced to categories. Second, due to a restriction of range, this "lost information" reduces power and the chances of obtaining statistical significance when utilizing samples of equal size. There may be meaningful differences among dyads that go undetected because the original scores were "condensed" into narrowly defined categories.

It is not easy to interpret discrepancy scores. Some researchers (Deal, Halverson, & Wampler, 1989; Kenny & Acitelli, 1994) emphasized that these indices do not necessarily reflect a dyad's characteristic: if a dyad shows a similarity between the two members in a specific construct, this

Table 2.1 A contingency table format

Level on the scale	Discrepancy score		
	High	*Medium*	*Low*
Both high	a	b	c
Mixed	d	e	f
Both low	g	h	i

similarity could be imputed to an effective commonality between the two members due to their specific relationship or to their culture; in other words, the two members answered in a stereotypical way, according to the prevalent culture. The problem with the interpretation of these indices is in the lack of a random group that allows us to determine whether the dyadic score could be attributed to the specific relationship/family or is casual. Glass and Polisar (1987) suggest creating a sample constituted by casual dyads ("pseudocouples"), that is, couples formed by subjects who have no relationship with each other. This procedure makes it possible to verify whether the dyadic scores in a family are really different from the dyadic scores in the pseudocouples. According to Kenny (2000), this procedure could suffer as a result of the way in which couples are constituted: it requires creating various casual dyad samples and verifying that the dyadic score does not vary too much. Kenny and Acitelli (1994) proposed some data-analysis strategies that allow us to disentangle the score from the stereotypical effect. For example, in a marital dyad the male stereotypical effect is the mean of the husbands' score on item *i*, and the female stereotypical effect is the mean of the wives' score on item *i*.

As we have already pointed out, no score is better than another but every dyadic score is able to capture only some of the dyad's characteristics. To obtain indications about the best type of score to use, Larsen and Olson (1990) propose calculating the Pearson's correlation and the paired *t*-test. They then suggest creating a matrix like that reproduced in Table 2.2.

For instance, if in the case of scores from husbands and wives the *t*-test is not significant and the correlation is high, the scores from men and women are not different. In this case a suitable choice would be the mean. But if the *t*-test is significant and the correlation is low, this indicates that husbands' and wives' means are very different and a discrepancy score would be a better choice. Among the various dyadic scores there is no particular score that can render the complexity of the dyadic/family study. Each score makes it possible to consider a specific aspect of the dyad, apart from other aspects.

Another way to analyse family data is to create family typologies. The major benefit in this case is that each type summarizes the main characteristics of a group of families. There are both dyadic typologies and family typologies. In the first case, researchers might be interested in an *agreement/ disagreement typology*. Fournier, Olson, and Druckman (1983) built a

Table 2.2 Matrix depicting combinations of results between correlations
and *t*-test

Correlations		Paired t-*test*
High (*r* > .30)	Low (there is no difference between means): MEAN	High (there are differences between means)
Low (*r* < .30)		Very high difference between means: DISCREPANCY SCORES

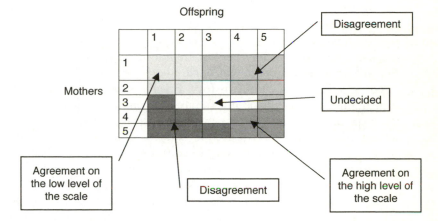

Figure 2.2 The typology of agreement/disagreement (Fournier, Olson, & Druckman, 1989).

dyadic typology by creating a contingency table in which mothers' scores appear in the rows and offspring's scores in the columns (Figure 2.2). In this way, it may be possible to distinguish the dyads in which there is a positive agreement from the uncertain dyads and the dyads characterized by disagreement. Agreement/disagreement typologies make it possible to distinguish different levels of agreement/disagreement, unlike the similarity/discrepancy scores previously illustrated.

This type of typology was used by Rosnati (1996) to analyse how family communication is related to agreement/disagreement between parents and offspring on future expectations (see Chapter 4).

Family typologies are desirable when a researcher intends to consider several points of view. Scabini, Lanz, and Marta (1999) used the means from each subsample as criteria to divide the score of fathers, mothers and offspring regarding family satisfaction. Then, by combining the codified data, we obtained eight family types. The study then focused on the two extreme types—satisfied and unsatisfied families—to test for the distinctive characteristics of the two types.

How to analyse data

As already mentioned, the second way to obtain relational/family data consists in choosing data analysis techniques that do justice to the peculiarities of relational data.

A central problem with data collected from multiple family members is that they are not independent and many techniques, such as regression and analysis of variance, require that data be *independent*. The *non-independence* of data relies on the assumption that people belonging to the same group are more similar than people belonging to different groups. Kenny and Judd (1986) emphasize three factors that give rise to the *non-independence* of data in groups: the compositional effect, common destiny, and reciprocal influence. In families, non-independence of data can result from compositional or non-random sampling effects: groups or families are not composed randomly and roles within families are not interchangeable (Scabini, 1995). Second, non-independence can come about because of a family or group's common destiny or shared history. Finally, social interaction may result in group linkage: members of a family or group continually interact with each other and their interactions produce a strong linkage that might be reflected in the data. Even if non-independence of data presents many problems during analysis, it is necessary to consider non-independence as a source of information. There are many occasions when non-independence is not a statistical problem to be overcome but is the fundamental issue that we are trying to understand, such as the relational nature of the family. So the point is to look for techniques that respect the relational nature of family data. One way to take into account the non-independence of family data is to maintain the dyadic/group unit of analysis. This is consistent with what has been shown so far. The participants in a study will not be individual subjects, then, but families: in this way, the data (families) will be independent from each other. What are the analytical techniques that allow us to compare different points of view? We will now describe examples of several research projects that we have conducted over the years using the following analytical methods. For further information about data analysis techniques, we refer the reader to the many existing texts on statistics (Stevens, 2002; Tabachnick & Fidell, 2001).

Gender differences in relations

Gender differences have to do with the differences between males and females in terms of perceptions of relations with parents, or the difference between mothers and fathers with respect to the relationship with a child. In the first case, a *t*-test carried out on independent groups is the most suitable statistical technique, while in the second case, due to the non-independence of the observations, a *t*-test on paired samples turns out to be more desirable.

Example 1

Aim: to analyse late adolescents' gender differences regarding communication with mother

Sample: 200 late adolescents

Unit of analysis: individual

Instrument: Parent–Adolescent Communication Scale (Barnes & Olson, 1982)

Data analysis: independent *t*-test

Results:

Table 2.3 Mean and standard deviation (s.d.) of daughter–mother and son–mother communication

	Mean	s.d.
Female	3.14	.82
Male	2.84	.75

$t(198) = 2.708 \ p < .01$

Because the *t*-test is significant, it is possible say that females perceive better communication with mother than males do

Example 2

Aim: to analyse mother's and father's perception regarding communication with a late adolescent child

Sample: 200 father–mother dyads

Unit of analysis: dyad

Instrument: Parent–Adolescent Communication Scale (Barnes & Olson, 1982)

Data analysis: paired *t*-test

Results:

Table 2.4 Mean and standard deviation (s.d.) of mother–late-adolescent and father–late-adolescent communication

	Mean	s.d.
Mother	3.51	.70
Father	2.96	.96

$t(199) = 9.29 \ p < .001$

Because the *t*-test is significant, it is possible say that mothers perceive better communication with their late adolescent children than fathers do

Generational differences

Differences in generations allow us to highlight the generational specificity in perceptions of relationships. The number of generations to compare will vary according to the unit of analysis chosen (dyadic, triadic, etc.). In the case of two generations—mother and child, for example—the statistical test to use to establish the comparison is the paired *t*-test whereas in the case of more than two points of view, it is best to use a within-subjects MANOVA.

Example 3

Aim: to analyse mother's, father's and late adolescent's perceptions regarding family satisfaction
Sample: 690 triads
Unit of analysis: triads
Instrument: Family Satisfaction Scale (Olson & Wilson, 1982)
Data analysis: within-subjects MANOVA
Results:

Table 2.5 Mean and standard deviation (s.d.) of mother, father and late adolescent family satisfaction

	Mean	s.d.
Mother	3.98	.54
Father	4.09	.55
Adolescent	3.73	.62

$F(2) = 14.81 \ p < .001$
The within-subjects MANOVA was significant, demonstrating that the perceptions of family satisfaction of mothers, fathers and children differed. The *post hoc* test (Bonferroni) reveals that children have a significantly lower perception than their parents

---

Relational predictors of well-being

Which perspective is best able to predict a child's well-being? The answer to this question can be found by using multiple regression. The use of multiple regression in family research, however, must take into account the multicollinearity of data. At times, in fact, the data from fathers, mothers, and offspring turn out to be highly correlated, with the result that the regression technique is not applicable. This limitation may be overcome by using second-order data such as the discrepancy score, previously discussed, in order to limit elevated correlations.

Example 4

Aim: to verify the influence on adolescents' well-being exerted by different rela-
tionships in terms of agreement
Sample: 120 triads
Unit of analysis: family triads (father–mother–child)
Instruments: Parent–Adolescent Support Scale (Scabini & Cigoli, 1992), Self-Esteem
(Rosenberg, 1965); Self-Image Questionnaire (Offer, Ostrov, & Howard, 1981)
Data analysis: multiple regression analysis
Results: the discrepancy score was calculated for every relationship considered, as
described above. The three discrepancy scores are considered to be pre-
dictors of well-being in offspring.

Multiple regression shows that the only significant predictor is the discrepancy
between father and child, with a beta = $-.37$, $R^2 = .14$

CONCLUDING REFLECTIONS

Family research is intrinsically complex precisely because of its subject
matter. What and how we investigate are inextricably connected and it is
only by explicitly defining the link between the "what" and the "how" that
it becomes possible to understand the results obtained. Research results are
the effects of a process and can be gathered in different ways: it is therefore
indispensable to know how they were obtained to properly interpret them.
There is no right or wrong research on family relations but research can be
either consistent or inconsistent. Ensuring the consistency between the
various phases of a study is a challenge for researchers because it obliges
them to reflect on every detail of a project. We observed in Chapter 1 that
the starting point for studying the family consists in seeing it as a relational
object in which different relationships are organized. Difference becomes a
specific aspect in this research because it is at the very origin of the family:
we are referring to the differences between genders and generations. The
conceptual and methodological challenge for the researcher is to study
family relations while always keeping in mind the different levels present in
the family. No study can collect all the data, using various methodologies,
from all family members and system levels. There are compromises to be
made at every step of the research process, and it is important to identify
these limitations to understand fully what we are giving up as well as what

we are gaining. We study family relations in order to approach as closely as possible to an understanding of the family as something that is more than the sum of the relationships within it. In Chapter 1 we sought to define what the family is; in this chapter we have examined how we study the family, that is, which methodology comes closest to capturing the object under investigation. Numerous limitations are imposed by this object—the units of analysis and the non-independence of data—but this only makes research on family relations all the more fascinating.

Part II

An analysis of family relationships by gender and generation

3 Parents and children face to face: an analysis of relations and family functioning by gender and generation

INTRODUCTION

In the next two chapters we present data from studies carried out over the past 15 years by researchers at the Centre for Family Studies and Research. This research shares the *same goal,* to study relations in families with late adolescents and young adults, the *same fundamental perspective*, the relational–intergenerational perspective (see Chapter 1) and, finally, the *same research "philosophy"* (see Chapter 2). More specifically, from a theoretical point of view, these projects all focus on relations in families facing the transition to adulthood, analysed in terms of gender and generation. From the perspective of research, they all employ at least the family triad for an analysis that we have defined as being relational. This allows the researcher to take into consideration genders and generations one at a time and, subsequently, to compare them. Therefore, the following presentation of research and related findings should be seen as the operative realization of the material covered in theoretical and empirical terms in the preceding chapters. This research will be compared to the results regarding the topics under examination as found in the international literature. The findings that we are about to describe refer to various research projects conducted over the years and, therefore, to different databases. The descriptive data of each research project (acronym, sample, aims, instruments used, analyses) are outlined in the Appendix, while the following is a synthesis of the results. In the course of the past 15 years, our research has moved in two directions, in keeping with the national and international literature and the "latest fashions" proposed therein. First of all, we have undertaken the study of the parent–child relationship through variables that we can define as being "dyadic", that is, which probe perceptions having to do with the relationship between two family members with respect to one specific construct (for example, communication and support). Second, we studied family functioning through variables definable as being "global", in that they are used to investigate perceptions relating to the entire family organization (for example, cohesion and adaptability).

In the present chapter, we present data regarding the quality of relationships and family functioning. The next chapter will look at findings on the connection between, on the one hand, relations and family functioning and, on the other hand, risk or distress for the late adolescent and young adult, prosocial behaviour, and future planning. The ensuing paragraphs have been organized in such a way that a synthetic illustration of constructs under investigation is followed by an exposition of our research results. We first present results from the children's point of view, to be followed by those reflecting the parents' point of view and, finally, we compare the two perspectives in order to detect the elements that are either shared or different and, above all, to highlight the meaning and the "benefit" of a joint consideration of the viewpoints of two family generations.

It should be emphasized that in all the samples of the research presented here the children—whether late adolescent or young adult—were not married, still lived in the family home and were mostly students. It should also be pointed out that the family's socioeconomic status and the young person's status—whether student or employed—never turned out to be discriminant with respect to the psychosocial variables under investigation.

THE PARENT–CHILD RELATIONSHIP: AN ANALYSIS BY MEANS OF DYADIC VARIABLES

When studying the relationship between parents and children using "dyadic" variables, we essentially investigated support and communication, two constructs that are crucial to an understanding of the bond between generations in the family. The centrality of communication in family interaction has been attested to by numerous studies and models. Olson (1986) not only considers it to be at the core of family functioning, along with cohesion and flexibility, but also believes it "facilitates" family processes regulating intra- and interfamily distances. In the McMaster model (Epstein, Bishop, & Baldwin, 1982), communication is one of the six principal dimensions of family functioning. In Beavers' model of family competence (1982), it is implicitly given centre stage in that the author believes that autonomy is promoted by clearness of expression and family affectivity supported by the capacity to express feelings as well as emotional tonality. In the literature, communication has been investigated in terms of its openness and problematical aspects, on the one hand, and topics of conversation, on the other. Research on communication during the transition to adulthood shows that parents experience greater satisfaction in communication than their children, in the sense that they perceive communication to be more effective and less conflictual than their children do (Cicognani & Zani, 2003; Noller & Callan, 1990; Youniss & Smollar, 1985). Numerous studies reveal significant differences in parent–child communication with respect to the gender of either the parent or the child. The younger generation exhibits more openness with their mothers and prefers their advice on issues having to do with themselves, the social context, the family, school, and questions about the meaning of life. With fathers, however, late adolescents seem to have greater difficulty in communication and are more defensive and selective in the choice of topics to discuss. As to children's gender, the results are still contradictory but there appears to be good evidence to support the existence of a privileged axis of communication between mothers and children, especially between mothers and daughters. Along with communication, parental support is considered to be one of the most robust variables in the socialization of offspring.

Social support has been variously defined (Williams, Barclay, & Schmied, 2004) and measured (Cohen, Underwood, & Gottlieb, 2000). It is a multidimensional construct and several supportive functions have been discussed in the literature. Specifically, these have mainly been: emotional support, instrumental support, informational support, companionship support, and validation (Wills & Shinar, 2000).

In our conceptualization, we have defined support as knowing that we can "count on" another person or, in other words, as the reliability of the bond (Scabini & Cigoli, 2000). To some extent, our conceptualization of support might be considered as a definition of the emotional function of support (Burleson, 2003), but the specificity of our definition is that support was conceptualized as a fundamental characteristic of the relationships and, for this reason, it is a dyadic construct and relational specific.

Starting with the literature, therefore, and by means of cross-sectional studies conducted over the years (see the Appendix: databases in Table 1— B. FRAP, 1994; D. YAPI, 1996; E. LAYAF, 1997; F. LAF, 1998; I. CATA, 2000), we have investigated how communication and support vary during the different phases of the transition to adulthood. Moreover, we have examined its quality in terms of communicative openness, problems, and content as revealed through the perceptions of parents (fathers and mothers) and offspring. The data have always been analysed in terms of "gender and generation".

The children's point of view on communication and support

Research we have carried out in the past 15 years with different databases has produced results that have not changed over time with respect to the variables of communication and support. The late adolescents and young adults (aged 16–30) who have participated in our studies have obtained medium to high scores on the variable of *communication* with fathers and mothers: this points to the existence of dialogue in these families that offers the possibility of freely expressing and sharing ideas and opinions, as well as indicating low levels of problems in communication. The instrument used to detect the quality of parent–child communication is Barnes and Olson's (1982) Parent–Adolescent Communication Scale (PACS; Box 3.1). This finding concurs with the international literature on the subject and remains constant over time and in all phases of transition to adulthood.

Box 3.1

Parent–Adolescent Communication Scale (PACS)

This instrument consists of 20 *items* subdivided in two subscales. The first, composed of 10 *items*, measures *openness* in parent–child communication, that is, the freedom in the exchange, the degree of understanding and satisfaction experienced in the interaction; the second, also of 10 *items*, assesses to what extent communication is problematical, that is, the absence of sharing, negative interactive style, and selectivity of topics discussed. The two subscales are summed, thus obtaining a global index of the quality of communication between parents and children. Responses to the PACS are based on a 5-point Likert scale (from "very much in agreement" to "very much in disagreement"). The Italian version of the instrument was tested on a sample of 1120 adolescents and their parents (Lanz, 1997). The subjects' scores on the scale, when subjected to a factorial analysis, produced the same factors as Olson's original instrument. Cronbach's alpha, used for an analysis of the scale's reliability, equals .82. The adolescent completes two versions of the scale: the first in reference to father, the second in reference to mother. Examples of items regarding openness in communication are: "My father/mother/child is always a good listener", "When I ask questions, I get honest answers from my father/mother/child". Examples of items measuring the existence of problems in communication are: "There are topics I avoid discussing with my father/mother/child", "I don't think I can tell my father/mother/child how I really feel about some things".

Another finding that cuts across all the databases of late adolescents and young adults in our research has to do with late adolescence: this, the most critical phase of transition to adulthood, witnesses an increase in problematical aspects and a decrease in openness in communication with fathers and mothers. A likely explanation is that young people, involved in the construction of their own identity and the process of differentiating themselves from their parents, set clear limits around their life space in order to distinguish themselves from the significant others in their lives. More specifically, boys and girls communicate with their parents in different ways. All datasets clearly and explicitly point to the existence of a privileged axis of communication between mothers and daughters and one between fathers and sons, regardless of the children's ages.

What do Italian late adolescents and young adults talk about? The most common topic of conversation between parents and children (in which the mother is the preferred interlocutor of both sons and daughters) is extra-familial achievement (school or work) and future plans. As database F. LAF (1998; see Appendix Table 1) has shown, for example, "future choice" is discussed frequently/fairly frequently by more than 80% of the sample with mother, and by more than 70% of the sample with father, with obvious differences between males and females that confirm the pattern previously described (Scabini, 2001). In terms of *support*, children's perceptions also reveal differences linked to age: early adolescents perceive a higher level of support than middle and late adolescents do (database F. LAF, 1998; see Appendix Table 1). The instrument used to detect the quality in parent–child support is Scabini and Cigoli's (1992) Parent–Adolescent Support Scale (PASS; Box 3.2).

Box 3.2

Parent–Adolescent Support Scale (PASS)

This instrument is composed of 13 items, based on a 5-point Likert scale, that are used to analyse the reliability of the bond between parents and the adolescent. This scale investigates the level of support, i.e. how much an adolescent can count on his/her parents. It has shown a good alpha in the Italian sample (1378 subjects, late adolescents and adults) on which it was tested, e.g. 95. Each subject provides responses on a 5-point Likert form. Adolescents complete two versions of the scale, focusing on the support existing between themselves and their mothers in the first version, and their fathers in the second. Examples of items measuring the existence of support are: "I can count on my father/mother when I need something", "My father/mother understands me" (adolescent version).

Likewise for communication, mother is the parent perceived by late adolescents and young adults as being closest (databases F. LAF, 1998; I. CATA, 2000 in Table 1 of the Appendix; Lanz, 1998; Scabini, 2000); however, in contrast to communication, no differences due to offspring's gender were found for this variable.

In brief . . .

- On the whole, late adolescents and young adults perceive communication with their parents to be good, very open and largely problem-free; they also perceive a highly supportive relationship with both parents.
- Late adolescents and young adults perceive the relationship with their mothers to be better, more open and supportive than with their fathers (Lanz, 2000; Scabini, 2000b; Scabini & Marta, 1995).

- Late adolescent males perceive better communication with their fathers than females do, and late adolescent females perceive better communication with mothers than males do (Scabini & Marta, 1995).
- Late adolescents (both male and female) perceive more problems in communication with their fathers and mothers than young adults and early and middle adolescents do (Lanz, 2000).

This picture undergoes variations when we examine parent–child relationships in families that are facing particularly critical transitions. In our work we have given particular consideration to families in which the children were adopted or in which the parents are separated or divorced.

The way in which relationships between parents and children are managed is a crucial issue in separated families and adopted families. When the children concerned are late adolescents, special problems may arise since transition to adulthood is usually considered a phase of particular vulnerability for parents and their offspring, whether separated, adopted or non-adopted (Aro and Palosaari, 1992; Hauser, Vieyra, Jacobson, & Wertlieb, 1985; Hetherington, 1991; Mackie, 1985; Scabini, 1995). Separated families and adoptive families with adolescents have to cope not only with the challenges of this particular phase of the family life cycle, but also with a unique set of developmental tasks stemming from their status.

The children of divorce in our research came from families in which parental separation had occurred from 1 to 16 years before the study began (mean 7.5 years). Of these children, 90.2% were living in single-parent families with their mothers and 9.8% with their fathers. The data for fathers always refer to the natural father.

Regarding adoptive families, all the adopted late adolescents had been born in a foreign country and adopted by an Italian family when they were aged from 0 to 11 years; the mean age at adoption was 4.3 years. In total, 62.4% were born in Latin American countries (e.g. Brazil, Chile, or Bolivia), 31.2% in Asia (e.g. India or Sri Lanka) and 6.4% in Eastern European countries (e.g. ex-Yugoslavia).

A comparison of these types of family with biological families reveals significant differences in both communication and support. As a matter of fact, comparative analyses of databases (FRAP-BIOADO, 1996; PACASE-TYPA, 1999; see Appendix Table 2) with children from intact, biological families and adopted children have shown that adopted children tend to assess the quality of relations with parents, particularly as regards communication, more positively than their peers in biological families do (Lanz, Iafrate, Rosnati, & Scabini, 1999). More specifically, adopted children perceived a lower level of problems in communication with their mothers than biological children did, and the same level of openness and support (Rosnati & Marta, 1997). Adopted children judged communication with their fathers to be more open and less problematical than their non-adopted peers did. On average, they perceived the same level of support. Adopted children perceived greater openness in communication with mothers than with fathers but with the same level of problems, while their biological counterparts rated communication with mothers to be significantly more open and less problematical than with fathers. Furthermore, differences in the level of support appeared only in the biological sample. Adopted children felt that they had an equally supportive relationship with both parents, while their peers living in biological families perceived a more supportive relationship with mothers than with fathers.

The analysis of the data demonstrates that children from divorced parents have more difficulties in the relationship with both father and mother than children from adoptive and biological families, and that adoptive children generally perceive a more positive relationship with parents than their peers do.

The parents' point of view

Now let us turn to findings reflecting parents' perceptions. With respect to *communication*, both parents feel they experience good communicative exchanges with their children, marked by a high degree of openness and low levels of problematical aspects. There are clear differences between parents, however, in that mothers believe they have better communication with their children than fathers do. Parents also obtain medium to high scores in support. However, fathers and mothers report similar perceptions of support towards their child, whether this is a son or daughter, and this perception does not change with the transition from late adolescence to young adulthood. In other words, while for offspring the transition to adulthood is marked by critical moments that function as turning points, parents perceive it as a uniform period of time: parents thus seem to have difficulty modifying aspects of the relationship that are most closely connected with the bond and the sense of belonging.

In brief . . .

- On the whole, parents perceive communication with their children to be good, very open and largely problem-free; they also experience highly supportive relationships.
- In terms of communication and support, parents do not perceive different relations with offspring with respect to gender or age.

The findings discussed so far, which relate to biological parents belonging to intact biological families, become more interesting if they are compared to findings obtained for adoptive parents and separated or divorced couples, reminding us of similar findings for offspring. Mothers and fathers in adoptive and non-adoptive families judged communication with their children to be of the same quality as in biological families with one exception. Adoptive mothers perceived more problems in communication with their children than biological mothers did. Furthermore, adoptive parents assessed relations with their children to be more supportive and reliable than their biological counterparts did. No difference was found between adoptive mothers and fathers in support levels while non-adoptive mothers perceived that they had a more supportive relationship with their children than their husbands did (Rosnati & Marta, 1997). No significant differences emerged between broken and intact families in either parent's communication with a child (Scabini, 2001).

Comparing parents and children

In this section we elaborate on our analysis of the findings that are the fruit of an intergenerational perspective: in other words, we compare the "voice" of children with the "voice" of parents, in the hope of shedding light on the interwoven dialogue connecting the two generations. In terms of *communication*, this comparison makes it possible to assert that, in the families that comprise our databases, all members perceive good communication, even if this does not mean that all share the same perceptions. Significant differences are not lacking, whether between the two generations of parents and offspring or between genders—sons–daughters, fathers–mothers. As a matter of fact, parents perceive better communication with their children than the latter do. This result is consistent with the outcomes of Italian and international research on communication in families with adolescents and young adults: the children seem to be more critical, or perhaps more realistic, in describing communicative interaction with parents (Barnes & Olson, 1985; Hartos & Power, 2000; Jackson, Bijstra, Oostra, & Bosma, 1998; Noller & Callan, 1991). This finding is also confirmed with regard to support. Parents and offspring have differentiated perceptions of their own bond (Scabini, 2000b): in particular, parents perceive a higher degree of reciprocal support and this does not change over time. From their point of view, the bond with a child turns out to be reliable, if somewhat static, in the sense that parents do not seem to perceive any change with the passing of time. Offspring, for their part, assess the relationship with their parents as providing a lower level of support but have a more dynamic vision of the relational context and, with time, report an increase in the quantity of the support exchanged in the relationship. Therefore, according to their perception, from late adolescence to the phase of young adulthood,[9] there is an increase in the relational quality that coincides with entry into young adulthood. Likewise, our research shows that in young adulthood the indices of agreement between parents and children are higher than in the

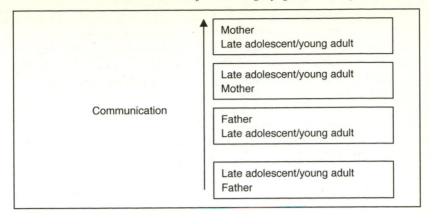

Figure 3.1 The ranking of the perception of parent–late-adolescent/young-adult communication.

preceding phases of the transition to adulthood (Scabini, 2000b). This means that, at the end of their voyage together as they approach the transition to adulthood, the two generations are closer: their perceptions are more harmonious with each other and are characterized by more support. Parents and offspring do share the perception, however, that the communicative exchanges between mothers and late adolescents and young adults are more "good natured" than those between fathers and their children. The position, in decreasing order, of the dyads of father–child and mother–child in terms of the congeniality of communication is as follows: mother's perception of communication with late adolescent and young adult; late adolescent's and young adult's perception of communication with mother; father's perception of communication with late adolescent and young adult; late adolescent's and young adult's perception of communication with father (Figure 3.1).

When we look specifically at late adolescents and young adults, the analysis of correlations between family members' communication scores produces an interesting result (Figure 3.2): males appear to have "coarser", that is to say, less refined perceptions than their female peers, who seem to be more sophisticated in managing relationships and more capable of discriminating within them. In short, while for boys their *own* perceptions about communication with father and mother are strictly correlated with each other, in the case of girls, their *own* perceptions about communication with a parent are more correlated with the perception of the *parent him-* or *herself* than with their own perceptions about the other parent. This attests to the fact that girls, in contrast to boys, give more importance to the aspect of *"reciprocity"* intrinsic to relationships and are not primarily motivated by what has been defined as the "principle of relational coherence", as stated by Sroufe and Fleeson (1988). Instead, they maintain the capacity to

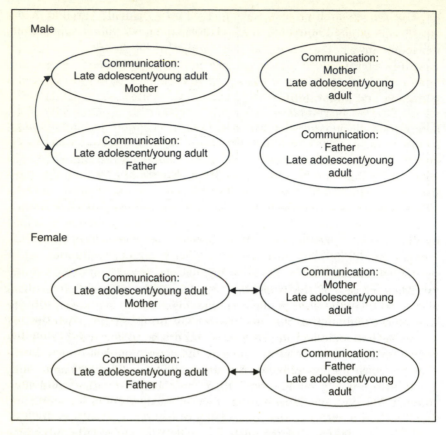

Figure 3.2 Correlations between family members by late adolescent/young adult
        gender.

differentiate between the maternal and paternal roles where boys tend to
conflate them: in their case, a good or bad communication with mother
predicts the same state of affairs in communication with father, while for
girls this does not turn out to be the case. In brief, the analysis by gender
and generation of the results of our research reveals the presence of some
common elements but above all of some very complex and differentiated
configurations between the members of families with late adolescents and
young adults.

FAMILY FUNCTIONING: AN ANALYSIS BY MEANS OF
GLOBAL VARIABLES

With respect to global variables, historically our research has focused on
cohesion and adaptability/flexibility and on family satisfaction. Recently,

some of our research projects have focused on a "global" variable that is cognitive in nature but treated in a "relational" manner: this is called family collective efficacy.

Cohesion and adaptability

The literature has focused much attention on cohesion and adaptability. Cohesion is an important family dimension. One of the most widely used models for studying this construct is Olson's Circumplex Model of Marital and Family Systems (Olson, Sprenkle, & Russell, 1979) and the most commonly used measures are those derived from it (the different versions of FACES, in the first place) (Cluff, Hicks, & Madsen, 1994; Farrell & Barnes, 1993; Green & Werner, 1996). In the Circumplex Model, cohesion is defined as "the emotional bonding that family members have towards one another" which includes variables such as "emotional bonding, boundaries, coalitions, time space, friends, decision-making, and interest and recreation" (Olson, 1993, p. 105). The extremes of the bipolar cohesion continuum (*enmeshed* versus *disengaged*) are hypothesized as being generally problematic. In line with Green and Werner, together with Barber and Buehler (1996) and Cox, Brooks-Gunn, and Paley (1999), we concur in believing that the construct *family cohesion* is more appropriately defined as shared affection, helpfulness, support, and caring among family members, while *enmeshment* refers to family patterns that facilitate psychological and emotional fusion among family members, "potentially inhibiting the individuation process and maintenance of psychosocial maturity" (Barber & Buehler, 1996 p. 433). Barber and Buehler (1996) have found cohesion to be a negative predictor of internalizing problems, such as depression and anxiety, and externalizing problems, such as delinquency and aggression, whereas enmeshment was a positive predictor of internalizing problems and of delinquency, but not aggression. In particular, it has been shown that family enmeshment has a negative effect on ego development (Best, Hauser, & Allen, 1997); individuality (Goldin, 1969; Kurdek, Fine, & Sinclair, 1995; Litovsky & Duserk, 1985; Steinberg, Lamborn, Dornbusch, & Darling, 1992); individuation (Barber & Shagle, 1992; Barber, Olsen, & Shagle, 1994; Costanzo & Woody, 1985; Smetana, 1995; Steinberg & Silverberg, 1986), and identity (Grotevant & Cooper, 1986; Hein & Lewko, 1994). According to this perspective, cohesion represents a positive side of family interaction and is linearly related to individual and family functioning (Cox et al., 1999; Maccoby & Martin, 1983). Research by Gavazzi (1993) has shown that optimally a family with adolescents will sustain both a high cohesion and a low enmeshment level, qualities considered to represent a high level of family differentiation (see also Cohen, Vasey, & Gavazzi, 2003). Cohesion is usually considered together with adaptability or flexibility. Adaptability is defined as "the amount of changes in [the system's] leadership, role relationships, and relationship rules" (Olson, 1993, p. 107), that is to say, the family's ability to change in response to situational and developmental stress. The findings produced by FACES III (Olson, 1986; Box 3.3) enable us to compute individual, couple, and family scores based on perceived-ideal discrepancy scores. As Olson pointed out, discrepancy scores may also be regarded as indicators of the desire for change: they provide information on how different family members see their family and how they would like it to be, that is, on how and in which way they desire their family to change with respect to cohesion and the adaptability level. This is the reason why we believe that these indexes may be assumed to gauge the propensity for change.

Box 3.3

Family Adaptability and Cohesion Evaluation Scale (FACES)

This instrument gives information about the perceptions and aspirations of both individual family members and the family as a whole. It is a 5-point, 20-item self-report measure. The scale consists of two subscales: cohesion and adaptability. The FACES scales are designed to allow for the classification of families as a function of their degree of cohesion, which can range from extremely low (disengaged), through moderate (balanced), to extremely high (enmeshed), and their degree of adaptability, which can range from extremely low (rigid), through moderate (flexible, structured), to extremely high (chaotic). It is administered in two formats: the perceived family ("How would you describe your family now?") and the ideal family ("How would you like your family to be?"). The standardized Italian version shows good reliability for both the subscales. Examples of items are: "Family members felt very close each other", " It is hard to know what the rules are in our family".

The literature reports that the perception of cohesion levels varies in relation both to one's gender and generation. These were the findings of a study carried out by Rossi and Rossi (1990) that examined adolescent–parent dyads and related that mothers rated cohesion more highly than fathers and daughters rated cohesion more highly than sons, resulting in the mother–daughter dyad reporting the highest rates of cohesion. It is possible that women use a different response set when assessing cohesion than men do; as such, their scores are inherently more likely to be similar on this dimension than on other dimensions or between other dyads. These findings are comparable to those of Graber and Brooks-Gunn (1999): in an examination of mother–daughter dyads, they found that mothers' and daughters' levels of cohesion are not significantly different.

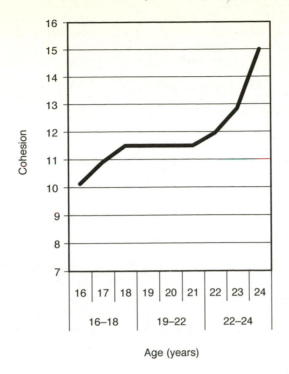

Age (years)

Figure 3.3 Progression of cohesion during transition to adulthood.

The children's point of view

Using Olson's FACES III, which explores representations of the perceived and ideal family, we have conducted numerous studies aimed at investigating cohesion and adaptability (databases A. YAF, 1988 and C. YOFCA, 1995 in Table 1 of the Appendix; Farina & Galimberti, 1993; Scabini & Galimberti, 1995). This research reveals that children perceive the real family as being characterized by intermediate levels of cohesion and high levels of adaptability. In the ideal family, young people desire an increase in adaptability. Consequently, children in this phase of the life cycle demand greater flexibility and social openness in their parents. Overall, children report a good perception of the perceived family, as revealed through the FACES, even if, during the period that spans adolescence, from 16 to 24 years of age, a particular progression is seen (Figure 3.3): the representations of the perceived family are at a good level—in slight but constant increase—from 16 to 18 years of age, but then undergo a period of plateau between 19 and 21 years to begin to rise again between 22 and 24 years of age. The data do not reveal differences imputable to gender.

In brief . . .

- Late adolescents and young adults have a good perception of their family (perceived family).
- Late adolescents and young adults desire more adaptability (ideal family).

Parents' point of view

An analysis of the findings obtained using the FACES shows that fathers and mothers perceive their own real families as being characterized by high cohesion and flexibility. It is interesting to note that parents desire an even more cohesive family (the ideal family). This is particularly true of mothers, who thus assume a centripetal role within the family system (Scabini & Galimberti, 1995).

The data reveal an effect of child gender on perceptions of family organization and propensity for change. Child gender partially explains the variance in family cohesion levels because there is a significant difference when the mothers' group was subdivided by the child's gender: cohesion levels are higher on average in mothers with daughters than in mothers with sons.

In brief . . .

- Parents perceive a high level of cohesion and adaptability (perceived family).
- Parents, especially mothers, desire more cohesion (ideal family).

Comparing parents and children

A comparison in terms of these variables reveals agreements and disagreements between genders and generations, as well. When it comes to cohesion and family adaptability, parents, unlike their children, desire an even more cohesive family. This is particularly true of family, especially mothers. The application of discrepancy scores (husband–wife; father–child; mother–child) on family members' scores are definitely interesting. Our datasets show that discrepancy in father and child cohesion and adaptability scores decreases as age increases. In order to connect the horizontal and vertical relationships present in the family, we conceptualized agreement in terms of distance. We were thus able to calculate intergenerational distance and compare it to marital distance, as far as cohesion is concerned. The results show that intergenerational distance (mother–child; father–child) and marital distance (mother–father) are closely connected and change with time: intergenerational distance increases in late adolescence while at the

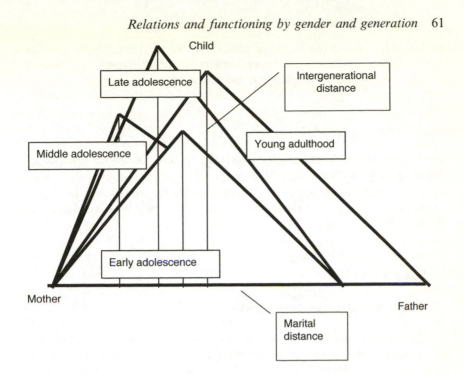

Figure 3.4 Family's configuration in the four groups.

same time marital distance decreases. In late adolescence the intergenerational distance reaches the maximum point. In the following phase, intergenerational distance decreases and marital distance increases. If we represent these findings graphically, we see that in terms of family cohesion, in families with young adults the triangle is equilateral (Figure 3.4). This is a general phenomenon on which child gender has no effect whatsoever. The narrowing of distance between father and child as a child's age increases confirms the tendency of intergenerational conflict to dissipate. In a sense, this also indicates a certain disengagement in the relationship itself or, at least, increased efforts to avoid stress. This is supported by the discrepancy between mother's and child's perceptions, which implies that continuing conflict and stress is probably caused by greater interpersonal contact.

Family satisfaction

Family satisfaction allows us to assess the subject's global judgement regarding the entire family: it is a global assessment of family relationships. It also seems to be an important and reliable indicator of family functioning. Satisfaction, although usually treated as a consequence of relationship, is also a cause (Hinde, 1988). The importance of this indicator lies in the fact that, as Cumsille and Epstein (1994) state, family satisfaction works as an individual cognitive appraisal and evaluation that late adolescents and their parents make of the family environment, "beyond the perceived characteristics of the environment itself" (p. 209).

The children's point of view

Late adolescents obtain medium to high scores on the global index of *family satisfaction* attesting to the situation of relational well-being present in Italian families in this phase of the life cycle (the instrument used to evaluate satisfaction is Olson and Wilson's (1982) Family Satisfaction Scale; FSS, Box 3.4).

Box 3.4

Family Satisfaction Scale (FSS)

This 14-item instrument is intended to assess family members' satisfaction. Application of factorial analysis (Principal Components Method) detected the presence of one factor. The reliability of the scale, measured on a sample of Italian late adolescents and parents composed of 1378 subjects, shows a Cronbach's alpha of .87. The 5-point response scale ranged from 1 (strongly disagree) to 5 (strongly agree). Example of the items are:

How well are you satisfied:
1. with how close you feel to the rest of your family?
2. with the way you talk together to solve family problems?

It should be pointed out, however, that the late adolescents most satisfied with their families are those from the higher social classes together with those who intend to continue their studies, as compared to the late adolescents who plan to enter the labour market directly after secondary school. Another variable that affects family satisfaction is late adolescents' *gender*: in our research, boys seem to be significantly more satisfied than their female peers (Scabini, 2001).

In brief . . .

- There is a good level of late adolescent satisfaction with the family during the transition to adulthood.
- There is a relationship between satisfaction and social class: satisfaction is greatest in families with more economic and cultural resources.

Parents' point of view

As far as the global index of *family satisfaction* is concerned, once again the scores are in the medium to high range and fathers, in particular, claim to be more satisfied than mothers. Family satisfaction in fathers and mothers does not vary with the successive phases of transition to adulthood nor with respect to offspring's gender.

In brief . . .

- There is a good level of parental satisfaction within the family during this phase of the family life cycle.
- Fathers are more satisfied than mothers.

Comparing parents and children

Family satisfaction, considered as a global index, is quite elevated in families with late adolescents and young adults, indicating a positive overall judgement regarding these families. In general, our findings very definitely suggest that the "adult" generation is more satisfied than the generation of children: fathers are the most satisfied family members, followed by wives, then young adult offspring and finally, late adolescent offspring. Subsequent to an analysis of the general findings and focusing first on single generations and then with a comparison between generations, we used database F. LAF (1998; see Appendix Table 1) to ascertain whether it was possible to identify a typology of global family functioning in the sample of families that connects some of the most salient elements to have emerged (Scabini et al., 1999). To this end, we used family satisfaction as the critical variable. Family typology was constructed using data from fathers, mothers, and children. The typology provided for the division of the family members' scores into two groups, adopting as criteria the mean scores and, specifically, each group's placement above or below the mean scores. Each of the three samples (mothers, fathers, and children) was divided into two subgroups: (1) one that scored below the sample group's mean score (low satisfaction); (2) one that scored above its mean score (high satisfaction). Crossing data from parents and children, an 8-type typology was constructed. The study focused on the two extreme types of the typology: the type called "families with adequate functioning or satisfied families" ($n = 186$), that is to say, families in which all the family members obtained scores above the mean score of their group and one called "families with inadequate functioning or dissatisfied families" ($n = 169$), that is, families in which all members obtained scores below the mean score of their group. These two types of family were compared according to crucial variables such as parent–child communication, topics of parent–child communication, family decision-making processes on topics related to the transition to adulthood, youths' freedom and youths' future orientation. An analysis of the typology found that:

1. Family satisfaction is without doubt closely related to good quality in the communicative exchanges between parents and children. Evidence for this is found in the fact that in satisfied families all the topics of conversation mentioned are addressed significantly more frequently than in dissatisfied families. In the latter, parents do not appear to function as reference points for their children—as guiding lights, in other words. Therefore, their children find themselves experiencing the process of growth in solitude and uncertainty, broken only by the advice of peers or occasional and/or sporadic interventions on the part of an adult generation that does not manage its hierarchical role in a clear and coherent manner. Perhaps we can attribute to this situation the importance that peers and their opinions assume for these young people.

2. "Satisfied" families appear to be characterized by shared perceptions, by a sort of "balance" in the roles played by parents, by parent–child relationships marked by communicative interaction, by the granting of freedom combined with sharing, and by the perception of parental support and confidence in the future due to the knowledge on the part of the younger generation that they can find within the family both stimuli for experimentation and elements of reassurance. In general, the data reveal that in satisfied families children have the impression of being able to make independent decisions, but also know that they can count on parents who make themselves available as reference points and who accept responsibility as parents to solve the problems their children may face. Such a context is positive for the child's development and for his/her progress towards differentiation from the family because it satisfies both a need to explore as well as a continuing desire for reassurance and protection (Scabini, 1995). At the other extreme, we find the "dissatisfied" families characterized by a lack of perceptive uniformity. The parental couple is less united at its core, occupies positions of greater divergence, and exhibits a relational imbalance towards the mother.

3. It is therefore to be presumed that satisfied families are able to fulfil their responsibility in this phase of life by carrying out their principal task of providing flexible protection for their children and by assuming a mediatory function with respect to the social domain as they find individualized strategies of inclusion within it. Dissatisfied families, on the other hand, have difficulty in understanding how to carry out this task. In other words, we can affirm that the former act as protective factors for young people and seem to have sufficient resources for

Table 3.1 Characteristics of satisfied and dissatisfied families

Satisfied families	Dissatisfied families
Parents share with their children the same perceptions regarding communication	Each family member holds different perceptions regarding parent–child communication
Regarding the decision-making process, the "sharing" option—at the same time, a communicative one (we discuss together) and a supportive one (we make the decision together)—is more used	Regarding the decision-making process, "total autonomy" and "limited autonomy" are more frequent
Adolescents receive the same amount of freedom from mother and father	A different parental behaviour regarding the amount of freedom is frequent
Parents not only know what their children want for their future, but also, in the great majority, are in favour	Parents don't know their children's future hopes and plans
Adolescents are more certain regarding their future	Adolescents are less certain regarding their future
Father is the mediating figure between the family and the social context	Peers are the mediating figures between the family and the social context

facing their transition to adulthood, while the latter appear to be searching for strategies to come to terms with this difficult phase in the life of a family (Table 3.1). Data from our research, confirming an expected result, show that, with respect to *family satisfaction*, parents and offspring who belong to intact families obtain higher scores than parents and children in broken families (Scabini, 2001).

Family collective efficacy

Beliefs about family collective efficacy (Caprara, Regalia, Scabini, Barbaranelli, & Bandura, 2004; Zaccaro, Blair, Peterson, & Zazanis, 1995) reflect the judgements that family members make about the capacity of the entire family to operate as a whole system in accomplishing tasks necessary to family functioning. While other *self-efficacy* beliefs mostly concern dyadic relationships (parent–child; husband–wife) (Caprara, Regalia, & Bandura, 2002; Regalia, Pastorelli, Barbaranelli, & Gerbino, 2001), family collective efficacy beliefs focus on the perceived operative capabilities of the family as a whole. In reality, when focusing on family functioning, beliefs in one's personal efficacy alone may not be sufficient to ensure achievement of desired goals, nor can spouses, parents, and children fulfil their role requirements independently from other family members' feelings, expectations, and behaviours, as many outcomes are achievable only when all family members pool their resources and efforts together. In the family, as in any other social system, perceived collective efficacy affects the system's sense of mission and purpose, the strength of its members' commitments to what it seeks to achieve, how well its members feel they are able to meet their mutual obligations, and the family's resiliency in the face of adversities (Bandura, 1997). Family collective efficacy thus includes the family's ability to achieve consensus in decision-making and planning, to promote reciprocal commitment, to provide emotional support in difficult times and stressful situations, to keep good relations with relatives and the community at large, and to enjoy being together. The instrument used to evaluate family collective efficacy is Caprara et al. (2004), Family Collective Efficacy Scale (Box 3.5).

Box 3.5

Family Collective Efficacy Scale (FCES)

The Family Collective Efficacy Scale measures family members' assessment of their family's capacity as to the realization of a number of fundamental tasks for its good functioning and for the promotion of reciprocal growth. The scale, comprising 20 items with responses based on a 7-point Likert scale, focuses on the family as a social system composed of a set of interconnected relationships. The results obtained for the parents' group confirmed the monofactoriality of the scale. The reliability of the scale is very high: Cronbach's alpha is equal to .97 for both parents and children. Examples of the items are:
   How well, working together as a whole, can your family:
1. set aside leisure time with your family when other things press for attention?
2. help each other to achieve their personal goals?

Children's point of view

Children's mean scores on the scale are very high. No differences emerged between girls' and boys' scores. The collective family self-efficacy scale shows significant correlations with some variables connected to family functioning. In particular, for both boys and girls the data show negative correlations with problems in communication and an aggressive conflict style towards father and mother; positive correlations were found with openness in communication, support, a conflict style tending toward compromise with fathers and mothers, the degree of control exercised over children by parents, and an overall perception of family satisfaction.

Parents' point of view

For parents, as well, the scores on the scale are quite high. Significant differences between fathers and mothers emerge in the scores for family self-efficacy. Fathers obtain higher scores on the belief in collective family self-efficacy than mothers do.

In the parents' sample, beliefs in family efficacy turn out to be correlated with a wide range of family functioning indicators. In particular, we found that these beliefs are more strongly correlated with positive indicators of the relationship with a child (openness and conflict style based on compromise) and with family satisfaction than with variables that express relational tension (such as problems in communication and an aggressive conflict style). The direction of these correlations reproduce the findings already discussed relating to the children's sample.

Parents and children face to face

Parents' beliefs in family efficacy are only moderately correlated with the efficacy beliefs of their children. This is an interesting result and agrees with a great deal of the literature. It attests to the fact that offspring's and parents' perceptions of family relationships can be only partially superimposed. Being part of the same family does not mean that the different generations hold the same beliefs about knowing how to adequately manage family bonds. Each generation develops family efficacy beliefs that probably function above all to mark and document aspects of differentiation from the other generation. This is thus in keeping with the relational characteristics that denote the phase of the life cycle that parents and offspring are going through.

THE FAMILY CHORUS: GENDERS AND GENERATIONS FACE TO FACE

A theme that has been gaining prominence in family studies has to do with bonds and intergenerational dimensions or, put another way, consists in analysing relationships within the kinship network (see, for example, the classic works of Bengston and his group on the "intergenerational stake": Bengston & Achenbaum, 1993; Bengston & Cutler, 1976). The intergenerational bond can be defined as "the affectively invested web of meaning that connects multiple communal domains in the temporal dimension (history), each of which is in turn structured around symbolic meanings, rules, codes, operations and idiosyncratic outcomes" (Scabini & Cigoli, 2000, p. 32). Characterizing the family as the space where exchange between generations and genders takes place and focusing on intergenerational bonds—on what lies *between* the generations—means studying not only or primarily the stage where relational exchanges are played out but also, and above all, the intermediate space concealed by people's *actions*—whether those of fathers or sons, or of mothers or daughters—that will affect generations to come. Taking this into account means seeking agreements and disagreements in the actions carried out by the different generations and attempting to understand whether, and how, the actions of preceding generations could be connected to those of present generations. The data demonstrate how the understanding of relationships and family functioning is enriched by the study of multiple generations, with the factor of gender always taken into account as well.

The databases at our disposal clearly demonstrate that the perceptions of mothers and fathers convey even more emphatically than those of their children the image of a harmonious, conflict-free family characterized by good parent–children relationships and middle to high satisfaction with the family. It is important to note that fathers and mothers of late adolescents and young adults do not perceive differences in their relationships with their children due to age or gender (measured here in terms of communication, support, and family satisfaction): what seems to be most important for parents is the children's role. Parents thus show difficulty both in perceiving changes in their offspring over time and in clearly perceiving differences connected with their child's gender. All the databases indicate that mothers are at the centre of family bonds: their communication and, in general, their relationships with their children turn out to be more satisfying than the relations between fathers and offspring. Children discuss affective and relational issues with their mothers: in other words, the entire "private/inner" sphere is the domain of mothers. The data indicate beyond a doubt that the Italian scenario is characterized by families in which we observe a relational imbalance towards the mother. The numerous studies that we have conducted show that the mother is the fulcrum of family life. In families, and especially in satisfied families, the father also plays a pivotal role but in another sphere, that of the "social/outer" dimension. Children speak to their fathers about events in the news or concerning politics, they turn to him for advice about decisions for the future. In these families, a sort of realignment of the relational imbalance in favour of the mother takes place, thanks to the father's acceptance of his traditional role of mediator and interlocutor between the family and the social world. The coexistence of aspects that touch on both the affective and the normative registers and the "coherence" with which these manifest themselves in families with satisfactory functioning plays a very important role in the growth process of young people, who not only are able to measure themselves against a man or woman who conveys clear and well-differentiated sexual codes and models but can also see their interaction and interconnection. This is certainly an important family resource. It is very important that children have clear models of gender identification. This appears to be all the more critical for girls, who give evidence of a more tortuous and problematical growth process than boys. As a matter of fact, girls are less satisfied and experience greater difficulties in communication with their fathers. On the other hand, they show greater discriminatory capacities from the relational point of view. A conjoint analysis of these elements leads us to believe that the difficulty in which girls find themselves derives from the fact that they are truly "on the way" towards the transition to adulthood and that they wish to be active players in their own growth process, even if this causes events and relationships to become more problematical. For their part, boys show less tendency to create problematical family relationships. The perceptive differences between the generations with respect to family relations are evident. Offspring look at these relationships with a more critical eye: they are less satisfied than their parents with the climate in the family and with their communicative interaction with fathers and mothers. This is especially true for late adolescents, who seem to experience this phase as being more difficult and to have relationships more fraught with tension as compared to the preceding phases of the transition to adulthood and to the succeeding phase of young adulthood.

We should also note that the finding that adopted children perceive better relationships than their peers in biological families can be read as an attempt by adopted children to "more closely resemble" their parents: faced with the pain of an obscure birth, of abandonment and loss due to the death of parents and relatives, it is as if these children have a greater need of certainty in their identification with parents. However, this can lead to the risk that, in so doing, the process of distinction, typical of the transition to adulthood, will be impeded. It must be emphasized that for today's young people it is more important to have good family relationships than it was for their parents at the same age. This is the principal result of the comparison we carried out between parents and children in order to discover who are the significant others for present-day Italian late adolescents, and who were the significant others for their parents during their own adolescence (database B. FRAP, 1994; see Table 1 in the Appendix). In particular, we asked parents to imagine themselves as children and to indicate, in order of importance, who were the most significant persons for them when they were the same age as their own offspring. At the same time, we asked their late adolescent children to indicate who are the most significant figures in their lives right now. Our findings revealed that parents are the most significant others for both the present and past generations of late adolescents: father and mother are put in first or second place in the list of significant others by both generations. A more detailed analysis revealed the central position of the mother for both generations: now, as in the past, the mother is the principal reference figure from whom children seek advice, help, and support (Lanz et al., 1999). However, discrepancies emerged about the relative importance of other significant adults. Contemporary late adolescents seem to rely exclusively on their parents or, in their absence, on their peers, while the late adolescents of the past (i.e. the late adolescents' parents) could also count on the support of adults outside the family, for example, a teacher, a youth counsellor or a priest. These elements would not all have emerged if we had not taken into account the "conversation between generations", in other words, the musical counterpoint created by the voices of both generations that makes it possible to paint such a clear and complete picture of families with adolescents in transition to adulthood.

The importance of considering generations and genders will become even more relevant in Chapter 4, where family relations and functioning are considered in reference to risk for late adolescents and young adults, to their adopting prosocial behaviours, and to their capacity to plan for the future.

CONCLUDING REFLECTIONS

In this chapter we have analysed the quality of family relationships by intersecting different generational levels—inter- and intragenerational— with different genders and by using dyadic and triadic variables. The results for intact biological families were then compared with those for families in which parents are either separated or divorced and with adoptive families. This has allowed us to reveal just how varied and polyhedral the archipelago of family relationships during the transition to adulthood is, and how crucial it becomes for the research in this field to be increasingly attentive to the specific type of family context in which late adolescents and young adults live and to the "family paradigm" (Oliveri & Reiss, 1982). We are referring to all the assumptions a family shares about the fundamental nature of the social world—of each family and of each type of family.

4 Family relations, psychosocial risk, prosocial behaviour, planning for the future: parents and children face to face

INTRODUCTION

In this chapter we discuss the findings from our research of the last 15 years that take into account family relations as variables influencing or determining outcomes in the lives of late adolescents and young adults. We are referring to outcomes such as the development of a condition of psychosocial risk, that could inhibit the transition to adulthood. This is a precursor to deviance and is therefore of extreme interest from a preventive point of view. There are also outcomes that facilitate the construction of adult identity, such as involvement in volunteer work, a concrete prosocial behaviour that promotes well-being and integration into one's community. Finally, another outcome that facilitates the transition to adulthood is planning for the future, a necessary developmental task during this phase of life.

FAMILY RELATIONS BETWEEN RISK AND RESOURCES

There are a number of indications that we are currently witnessing a renewed process of change in the social structuring of the late adolescence and young adult phase. This means that adolescence and young adulthood as status-role configurations are becoming even more internally unbalanced and are increasingly characterized by inconsistencies, tensions, and a tendency towards disintegration; moreover, these phases are lasting longer and are generally losing their substantive form and structure. Various researchers have termed these developments the disappearance of youth (Gillis, 1993), the detraditionalization (Heelas, Lash, & Morris, 1996) or the destandardization of the youth phase (Biggart & Walther, 2001;[10] Perlman & Giele, 1983), and the individualization of youth biography (Beck, 1986; Furlong & Cartmel, 1997). As described in Chapter 1, the most important events in the transition to adulthood have generally lost their traditional collective character and gained an individualized quality (Hurrelmann & Chisholm, 1993). Taking into account the changing context of the transition, Biggart and Walther (2001) speak about "yo-yo transitions". This metaphor refers to the ups and downs, "either–ors" and "neither–nors" of young people today. Driving factors behind this yo-yo-ization of transitions are the restructuring of societies in terms of both flexibilization and individualization. Today's biographies swing, in the manner of a yo-yo, between dependency and autonomy: late adolescents and young adults may achieve legal or civil autonomy but still remain dependent on their family economically and in terms of cultural–emotional support. In particular, Biggart and Walther assess "the necessity of strong family support in the elimination of risk associated with modern youth transitions, according to the different cultural and institutional features that exist across Europe" (2001, p. 13). These changes in the transition to adulthood have endowed the family of origin with more value and influence (see Chapter 1).

The changing constellation of modern social life produces a changing set of challenges for young people, and hence a changing set of potential problems. Likewise, transformations in the structure and function of the family, which remains the social institution exerting the most control over the psychosocial development of humans across the life span (Amato & Keith, 1991), potentially pose challenges, as well as opportunities, for positive growth in the socialization of children growing up within these new family forms and, ultimately, for the future of modern society. In short, the transition to adulthood simultaneously takes on the connotation of challenge and resource for the entire family system: challenge in that it imposes numerous changes and relational transformations that the generations in a family may be unprepared to face or, for various reasons, unable to implement and accept; resource because it implies a "testing" of family functioning and the possibility of revising modalities of functioning that turn out to be non-adaptive. In the first case, the family could either fall into or reinforce behaviours and attitudes that, in the short or long term, may reveal themselves to be unfavourable to family members' growth; in the second case, the family could promote the resolution of difficult situations. In the words of Hauser and his collaborators (1985), the family can constitute a protective factor in facing risk and promote the transition to adulthood, thanks to the presence of *enabling* relations, those that facilitate the adolescents in assuming an adult role and autonomy. However, the family may also become a source of risk and inhibit development if it is characterized by *constraining* relations, those that are structured in such a way as to make the processes of differentiation and individualization difficult for adolescents (Hauser et al., 1985). In some of the less clearly illuminated sequences of the passages to adulthood, or in the passages themselves, we can detect constellations of factors that may bring about situations of risk (Chisholm & Hurrelmann, 1994). A risk constellation for the emergence of symptoms of psychosocial risk can be identified in the parent–child relationship (Cashwell & Vacc, 1996; Claes, Lacourse, Ercolani, Pierro, Leone, & Perucchini, 2001; Hoge, Andrews, & Leschied, 1996; Kerns,

Aspelmeier, Gentzler, & Grabill, 2001; Kirkcaldy, Siefen, & Furnham, 2003; Muris, Meesters, & van den Berg, 2003; Shek, 1997; Slonim-Nevo & Sheraga, 1997; Smetana, Crean, & Daddis, 2002). Among the risk factors highlighted by the literature in the parent–child relationship and in family functioning should be included poor communication, the absence of support, and a lack of family satisfaction. The presence of support and adequate communication is positively correlated with young people's individual and social adjustment (Barnes & Farrell, 1992; Barnes & Olson, 1985; Hess, 1994; Noller & Callan, 1990, 1991) and negatively correlated with deviant or delinquent attitudes. Moreover, some authors (Barber & Buehler, 1996; Cumsille & Epstein, 1994) state that young people's satisfaction with their families is associated with their adjustment and, in particular, with whether they develop depression. In any case, the literature teaches us that high family satisfaction can be correlated with good adjustment in young people and the resulting positive family climate can help young people in the processes of individuation and differentiation, which are fundamental to the transition and indispensable to becoming adult.

FAMILY FUNCTIONING AND OFFSPRING ADJUSTMENT

In accordance with a relational–intergenerational perspective and the research methodology consistent with it, in this chapter we take another look at the variables discussed in the preceding one, but this time they will be analysed in terms of their connection to psychosocial risk for the late adolescent and young adult. As usual, the point of view of late adolescents/young adults will be presented first, followed by that of parents and, finally, the two generations will be compared. Once again, children's and parents' gender will be of constant interest.

The children's point of view

Our studies (database B. FRAP, 1994, Table 1 in the Appendix; Carrà & Marta, 1995; Marta, 1997; Scabini & Marta, 1995) show that late adolescents' perceptions of support and openness in communication (with both mothers and fathers) are inversely related to psychosocial risk for adolescents, while the presence of problems in communication with mothers and fathers is directly related to this risk.[11] The mean scores for openness in communication and support increase from the low risk group to the medium risk group, and from this to the high risk group, while the mean scores for problems in communication decrease. No differences emerged between boys and girls in their perceptions of the relationship with their parents. The interaction between gender and risk does not appear to be significant.

   Moreover, children's perceptions of family satisfaction are also correlated in an inverse way with the risk for the children themselves. Furthermore, the

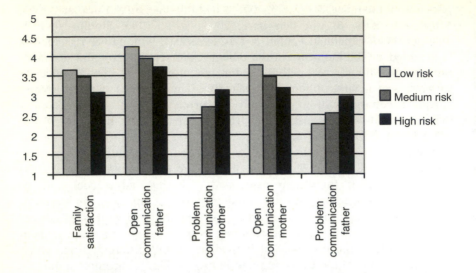

Figure 4.1 Family satisfaction, parent–adolescent communication perceived by
late adolescents by level of risk.

mean scores for family satisfaction decrease from the low risk group to the
medium risk group, and from this to the high risk group (Figure 4.1).

Late adolescents' psychosocial risk is affected by the quality of communication with fathers more than with mothers. As in the preceding
chapter, the picture changes when the data for late adolescents belonging to
so-called biological or intact families are compared with data for their peers
living in non-biological families, that is to say, for adopted children. As a
matter of fact, when the analyses were carried out on a sample of adopted
children and their parents, it became evident that a different pattern
emerged (Rosnati & Marta, 1997). The quality of communication between
adoptees and their mothers influenced their adjustment, while that with
fathers had no direct influence. For children in the adoptive subsample,
psychosocial risk is affected by the level of support that the adopted children perceived in the relationship with mothers, while the support in the
relationship with fathers had no direct influence. Thus, we can conclude
that the quality of father–child communication and the support from both
parents are important protective factors in preventing the maladjustment of
non-adopted late adolescents. On the other hand, the quality of the
mother–child relationship plays a crucial role in predicting adoptees'
psychosocial risk. The quality of the mother–child relationship in adoptive
families appears to be an important protective factor in psychosocial
adjustment during the transition to adulthood. The father, on the contrary,
plays a more important role in biological rather than in adoptive families in
determining the late adolescent's adjustment.

Regarding the collective family efficacy, children's scores show significant correlations with the indicators linked to children's psychological adjustment and maladjustment. In particular, collective family efficacy correlates in boys and girls in a positive and significant way with prosocial behaviour, satisfaction with life and optimism and in a negative and significant way with depressive states and violent conduct.

The parents' point of view

Let us now consider the data from parents. Fathers' perceptions of an absence of support and openness in communication and the presence of problems in communication are directly linked to risk for late adolescents. For mothers, only the perception of openness in communication is linked to a situation of risk for their children. For both mothers and fathers, perceptions about family satisfaction are linked in an inverse way with risk for late adolescents. When we look at the data from parents in the samples of adoptive families, no link emerged with regard to the support and communication perceived by both parents of adopted late adolescents.

Moreover, for biological parents, beliefs in family efficacy correlate with all the indicators of offspring's psychosocial adjustment. The most interesting finding has to do with the more decisive role played by fathers' beliefs in family efficacy as compared to those held by mothers for their impact on offspring's satisfaction with life, depression and, to a lesser degree, family satisfaction. The more fathers are convinced of their ability to manage relations with their offspring, the more their children experience high levels of family satisfaction, general satisfaction, and low levels of depression. This finding is coherent with the data from several studies recently carried out on family relations during the transition to adulthood, studies that document a "rediscovery" of the paternal figure and his centrality in determining the psychological well-being of his children (Doherty, Kouneski, & Erickson, 1998; Hosley & Montemayor, 1997; Lewis & Lamb, 2003; Risch, Jodl, & Eccles, 2004; Shulman & Seiffge-Krenke, 1997). Mothers' parental collective efficacy does not seem to play a specific positive role with respect to the prosocial conduct enacted by adolescents. The family self-efficacy of both parents exercises a protective function as regards the possibility that children might behave in violent ways.

Parents and children face to face

The scores from the scales measuring parent–child communication, parent–child support and family satisfaction completed by the fathers and mothers of different risk groups—low, medium, and high—were compared with those completed by their children. As a consequence of this comparison it emerged that the scores of perceived support and communication differ

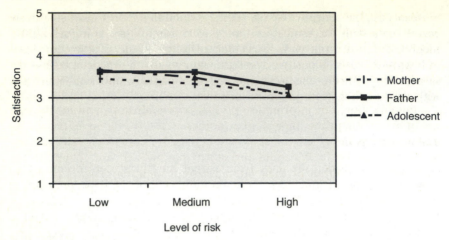

Figure 4.2 Family satisfaction perceived by mother, father and late adolescent by
level of risk.

significantly, most notably in the group with medium-risk scores. As for
family satisfaction, father–late-adolescent scores are different to a significant degree in the group at medium risk and mother–late-adolescent
scores differ in the group at low risk (Figure 4.2).

The discrepancy scores (see Chapter 2) were then calculated between
parents and children with respect to the two subscales for communication,
support and family satisfaction. In the total sample, the discrepancies in the
perceived support reported by fathers and late adolescents were correlated
with risk for late adolescents.

Conclusions

These findings, taken together, demonstrate that satisfaction, collective
family efficacy, support, and adequate communication appear to be important protective factors in preventing psychosocial risk in late adolescents and
young adults. But, even more importantly, the comparison between the data
from different genders and generations shows that the respective roles
of fathers and mothers emerge even more distinctly when we compare
parents' and children's perceptions of the extent to which a son or daughter
is at risk. It is precisely this comparison of findings for parents and children
that has enabled us to identify new features in family relationships. First of
all, our studies over the past few years have consistently shown that certain
variables—communication, support, and satisfaction—point to greater
agreement between fathers and children than between mothers and children.
Second, our research has shown that fathers are able to perceive different
levels of communication and support in relation to the level of risk that

children attribute to themselves, while the level of communication and support perceived by mothers does not vary according to their children's level of risk. If, as we saw in the previous chapter, the mother is the crucial reference figure in family relationships, our research shows that within the couple the father is the parent more able to grasp and understand the difficulties related by his child. We can therefore hypothesize that the father is a reliable source of information on family relationships and on the real condition of offspring. Indeed, the mother is less likely to notice problematic aspects in her relationship with her children, or to perceive distress signals (Marta, 1997). We could almost say that mothers are "blind" to the psychosocial condition of their late adolescent children. This is probably because mothers identify strongly with their children and therefore have greater difficulty in describing their family situation in a realistic way. These findings about fathers are very important from the practical perspective that focuses on preventing situations of distress from developing in the first place. They demonstrate that, although less socially visible and less easily detectable than that of the mother, the father's role is just as important precisely because fathers perceive more accurately their children's true condition. Moreover, the father's perception, more than the mother's, of family collective efficacy acts as a protective factor against risk for the late adolescent. Another important result is that late adolescents at a medium-risk level show more significant differences in scores with mothers and fathers about communication and support than late adolescents at low- and high-risk levels. It seems that while families with late adolescents at high and low risk neglect differences, in the first case, or use differences as a resource, in the second, families with late adolescents at a medium level of risk have not yet found a strategy for coping with differences. These families live "on the edge" between order and chaos and they seem to be trying to reorganize themselves by using trial-and-error strategies. In our opinion, late adolescents in this type of family are truly in a situation of risk. From the point of view of prevention, these families seem to have the greatest possibilities for change because their situation is fluid. For this reason, psychosocial prevention programmes would do well to address such families.

In brief . . .

- Satisfaction, support, adequate communication, and collective efficacy appear to be important protective factors in preventing psychosocial risk in late adolescents and young adults.
- Fathers and mothers assume different roles in promoting their children's well-being: fathers are reliable sources of information about their children's state of risk; mothers, overburdened with the tasks of child-rearing, seem affected by blindness with respect to their children's condition of risk.

FAMILY RELATIONS AND CONCRETE PROSOCIAL BEHAVIOUR: VOLUNTEERISM

Young people's prosocial behaviour is a topic that certainly stimulates psychosocial reflection in a time when there is growing concern in families, institutions, and civil society about the new generations and their existential, value-motivated, and behavioural choices, which are increasingly seen as problematical and potentially negative. Youniss (Youniss & Yates, 1997, 1999) was right to emphasize that there is a generalized judgement, or indeed prejudice, that the prolongation of the transition to adulthood produces mostly negative effects, in the sense that for the majority of young people the transition tends to resolve into a sort of latent state, an empty time in which choices and responsibilities that connote adulthood are put off to the future, instead of seeing this as a period of preparation for these choices and of a progressive assumption of responsibility. In reality, the universe inhabited by the younger generation reveals the presence of young people who, as they go through the transition to adulthood, accompany this experience with a choice in favour of solidarity, a choice they enact within volunteer organizations. Commitment to volunteerism carries with it a precise significance in the biographies of young adults: it has the potential to promote the development of personal and social identity (Grube & Piliavin, 2000). By means of action and commitment in the organizations they belong to, adolescents and young adults rediscover their past, impute new meanings to their existence in the present and develop hopes for the future. These are elements that can help young people along the path of identity construction, a path that requires the presence of peers, adults, and of meaningful contexts outside the home: all these can be found and become part of a young person's universe and life in the world of commitment and solidarity. The studies carried out on youth volunteerism have highlighted the positive effects of this type of commitment both on a psychological as well as social plane: it increases self-esteem and self-acceptance along with a sense of self-efficacy (King, Walder, & Pavey, 1970; Omoto & Snyder, 1990). It supports cognitive development, favours moral development (Yates & Youniss, 1996a, 1996b), and carries out a function of *empowerment* and support in identity construction (Amerio, 1996; Boccacin & Marta, 2003; Stukas & Dunlap, 2002). In addition, it functions as a protection from psychosocial risk (Benson, 1993), by working against adolescents' and young people's distress: this translates into a remission of behavioural disturbances, lower school drop-out rates (Moore & Allen, 1996), and a reduction in deviant/delinquent acts ending in arrests and imprisonment (Uggen & Janikula, 1999). It has been proven that volunteerism promotes socialization (Raskoff & Sundeen, 1994), political participation (Flanagan et al., 1999), civil involvement and support for prosocial norms (Kirkpatrick-Johnson, Beebe, Mortimer, & Snyder, 1998; Youniss & Yates, 1997). Therefore, it answers the needs for socialization and integration of young people into the social contexts. The volunteer group becomes the place where one can measure one's maturity and open up to the "human community" (Amerio, 2004; Cigoli, 1997). Thanks to participation in the volunteer group, the young person is able to see him- or herself as an active subject, responsible for his or her actions. Another effect of volunteerism highlighted by Youniss and Yates (1997) has been little discussed and studied but is nevertheless of extreme interest in that it relates to and questions not only the younger generation but also the adult generation from the exquisitely relational perspective of a reading of social phenomena. This view holds that volunteerism promotes an important *rapprochement* between the social generations, and the development of an intergenerational conversation through the experience of that which all young people hold in common: it offers the opportunity of a connection between oneself and society, and between the social generations, during the delicate phase of identity construction in which adolescents experience themselves as actors and agents but also need to be directed and guided by the preceding generation in order to best face the transition to adulthood. Volunteerism thus carries out a function of breaking the generational isolation within which young people and adults are confined, by promoting encounter and dialogue between the generations; it also contributes to expanding the family domain beyond its usual boundaries and promotes interchange not only between the individual and the community but also between the family and the community.

Notwithstanding the acknowledged importance of the family for the socialization of individuals and the documented influence the family exerts on at least two areas of volunteerism—political involvement and participation in groups with religious underpinnings (Janoski & Wilson, 1995; Pancer & Pratt, 1999)—studies that compare the choice to become involved in volunteer activity with family relations are scarce and of recent origin. These studies have demonstrated that some variables reflecting parent–child relations can promote or inhibit prosocial behaviour (one of the strongest determinants in volunteerism) and the commitment to volunteerism. These include authoritarian–democratic child-rearing styles (Eisenberg & Fabes, 1998; White, 1999), parental control and power being used in an appropriate way (Dekovic & Janssens, 1992), support (Csikszentmihalyi, Rathunde, & Whalen, 1993; Eisenberg, 1991; Eisenberg & Miller, 1987; Robinson, Zahan-Waxler, & Emde, 1994), warmth in parent–child exchanges and, finally, open and continuous communication, especially on topics relevant from the point of view of personal growth and a moral and social perspective. In particular, the most recent research (Fletcher, Elder, & Mekos, 2000; Pancer, Pratt, & Hunsberger, 1998) underscores the close connection between support, reinforcement/modelling, and parents' involvement in the community in promoting and predicting offspring's involvement or, put another way, as variables *of the intergenerational influence in the socialization of offspring to involvement in the social realm*. This is a finding that allows us to reread, articulate, and elaborate the relationship often described in the literature between community involvement and altruistic behaviours in the family, in particular on the part of parents, on the one hand, and, on the other, volunteer commitment in young people (Janoski & Wilson, 1995). As a matter of fact, if on one side research (Fletcher et al., 2000; Pancer, Pratt, & Hunsberger, 1998) shows that a coherent and constant reinforcement of involvement and prosocial behaviours, if not accompanied by commitment in the first person by parents, is not enough to induce young people to become involved in volunteerism, on the other side these studies also prove that the act of modelling, that is to say having parents involved in volunteerism, while offering young people a wealth of concrete and real opportunities to encounter and approach the context of volunteer commitment, to get to know it and become part of it, is also not enough to determine a conscious commitment. It should, moreover, be remembered that the majority of studies on the topic of volunteerism do not contemplate comparison with a control group. There is much research on the subject, in which some characteristics of volunteers are measured and evaluated as "absolute values" with no attempt to compare them to any sort of meaningful baseline. This approach, which is based on a prior assumption of volunteers' "difference", leads to very different results among the various studies in that, in the absence of a comparison, all the variables measured end up characterizing, in and of themselves, the group itself. In the following pages we will therefore analyse the family relations of those young people who have decided to live the transition to adulthood, and the uncertainty that characterizes it, when decisive life choices must be made (as we saw in Chapter 1), in a contextual way with an altruistic or prosocial experience, such as volunteerism. The research whose results we now present (database H. YAVOFA, 2000; see Table 1 in the Appendix) is designed so as to take into consideration a sample of family triads with a late adolescent/young adult involved in volunteerism and a sample of triads with late adolescents/ young adults not involved in any way in volunteerism, either in the present or the past. From a methodological perspective, the inclusion in the research design of a control group allowed us to define the salient traits belonging to the volunteer "figure", not apart from but starting with a "background" represented by individuals who, even if they exhibit similar socioanagraphic characteristics, did not choose to become involved in volunteer activity. Only in this way is it possible to discern at the same time analogies and differences between the variables measured in the two groups, thus defining the group of volunteers by means of truly characterizing traits.

The children's point of view

The presence of the control group in the research design allows us to affirm that family relations (parent–child communication in its dual aspects of openness and problems, parental support, conflict between parents and offspring, child-rearing style in its dual aspects of control and *laissez-faire*) in the young volunteers on the whole do not differ from their non-volunteer peers (Marta & Scabini, 2003). With a view to deepening our analysis of the young volunteers' family relations, we conducted analyses to check whether the volunteer's world should be considered as being monolithic, homogeneous, and undifferentiated, or whether it is possible to discern within it subgroups differentiated in terms of family variables (parent–child communication in its dual aspects of openness and problems, parental support, conflict between parents and offspring, child-rearing style in its dual aspects of control and laxity) and/or individual variables (prosociality in the young person, self-esteem, emotional insecurity), and/or sociostructural variables. To this end, a hierarchical cluster analysis was carried out using Ward's aggregate method on the following variables measuring family relations: parent–child communication, in the two aspects of openness and problems; parental support; parent–child conflict; child-rearing styles in the two aspects of control and laxity. The typology that emerged from the aggregation of the family variables was then related to the young person's prosociality, self-esteem, and emotional insecurity, and to sociostructural variables linked to volunteer involvement (the young person's gender and occupation, parents' income and occupation, the nature of the volunteer involvement engaged in, how the young person entered to become part of the volunteer group, motivations, changes produced by the volunteer activity engaged in, religious orientation).

These analyses revealed the presence of three clusters related to young volunteers' perceptions of the mother–child relationship as well as young volunteers' perceptions of the father–child relationship (Guglielmetti, 2003) (Figures 4.3 and 4.4).

The first cluster, which we may define as "conscious volunteers—modern donors" (the most numerous at 47.9% of the sample) groups together subjects characterized by good family relations with both parents, high levels of prosociality and empathy, and good self-esteem. This is the cluster that most clearly incarnates the prototypical positive characteristics of the stereotypic representation of volunteers. Besides exhibiting characteristics of adequate functioning, this cluster is made up mostly of females who come from families with a high income and with parents with middle to high educational levels. For the most part these young people are practising believers. Their motivations are divided between prosocial concerns and personal improvement—in spite of a slight predominance of the former, which is an indicator of good openness towards others together with a correct perception of the opportunities for personal growth offered by volunteer involvement. The perceived changes also exhibit an instrumental and, at the same time, reflective use of the activity these young people are engaged in. The second cluster, "volunteers by choice—searching for something" (35.8% of the sample) is a group that seems to have critical family relations. If the relationship with mother fluctuates around the middle range

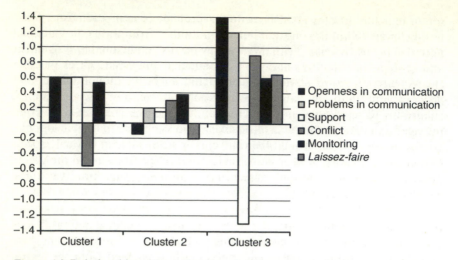

Figure 4.3 Relationship with mother perceived by young volunteers.

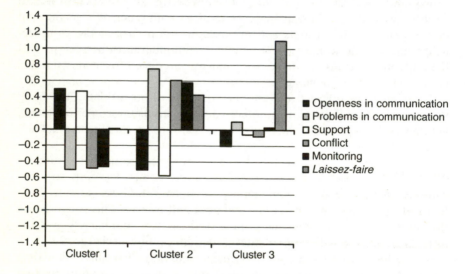

Figure 4.4 Relationship with father perceived by young volunteers.

(in which, however, her child-rearing style manifests itself in the form of moderate control), relations with father seem to be strongly imprinted with authoritarianism in terms of conflict, problems, and control in child-rearing. As to individual variables, the young people in this cluster have low self-esteem, high emotional insecurity but attest to the development of fair levels of prosociality. In this case as well, the subjects are mostly female, for the most part already involved in the working world, from families with middle to low socioeconomic and cultural status and stay-at-home mothers. This group is made up of a good percentage of religious non-practitioners and non-believers who became part of a volunteer group due to personal initiative in 50% of cases, with motivations mostly of personal improvement and growth, but that are also to a good extent prosocial. As in the first cluster, the changes perceived have to do with individuality but with a good dose of reflectivity, as well. Finally, the third cluster, "volunteers by chance—needing to belong" (equal to 16.3% of the sample), is characterized by very unbalanced family relations that are on the whole problematic. In this group, in fact, if relations with father seem to tend towards disengagement, those with mother are strongly marked by conflict and problems. Besides exhibiting low self-esteem and high emotional insecurity, the members of this cluster also seem to be characterized by prosociality that is well below the middle range. This is the cluster in which both sexes are equally represented and there is a good percentage of occasional volunteers whose involvement is less than 4 hours a week; many are students. Their families come from heterogeneous sociocultural backgrounds. A higher percentage than in the other two clusters occupies a decidedly low range of income and education but, at the same time, many parents turn out to hold a university degree and have a middle to high income. The common denominator of this cluster seems to be membership of parochial or otherwise religious groups that have promoted commitment to volunteerism. This is the cluster in which we find the greatest percentage of religiously active young people. Motivations derive from the world of values and community involvement more than from prosocial concerns and, at the same time, besides individual changes, there is evidence that volunteer commitment has led to a renewal of religious practice.

The parents' point of view

Turning now to parent–child relationships, we find that specific differences between the groups of parents of volunteers and non-volunteers cannot be discerned in terms of support, communication, and conflict. Significant differences emerge with respect to other variables, however (Table 4.1).

In agreement with the literature regarding individual variables, the young volunteers' mothers are more prosocial and hold more self-transcendent values than young non-volunteers' mothers. As to parent–child relationships and the relationship with the community, volunteers' mothers are less authoritarian and exhibit a greater perception of transmitting values to their children. They have more exchanges within the neighbourhood, are more involved in volunteerism, in political groups or associations, and are more commonly practising believers. According to the literature and Skoe's (1998) definition, it is mothers, as opposed to fathers, who carry the "ethics of care", that is to say, they are the custodians of prosocial needs, relational values, reciprocity, and the sense of social responsibility. Volunteers' fathers, as compared to non-volunteers' fathers, held fewer self-enhancement values,

Table 4.1 Distinctive elements of young-adult volunteer families versus young-adult non-volunteer families

Mothers
- More prosocial
- Carry more self-transcendent values
- Less authoritarian
- Higher perception of transmitting values to their children
- Greater exchanges within the neighbourhood
- Higher political engagement and involvement in associations
- More practising believers

Fathers
- Carry fewer self-enhancement values
- Less authoritarian
- More satisfied with their family of origin
- Higher involvement in associations
- More practising believers

are more satisfied with their family of origin, are less authoritarian, and are more committed to volunteerism. They also are more commonly practising believers (Marta & Pozzi, in press).

Family chorus

With the goal of understanding which variables of parents and of parent–child relationships are important in determining commitment to volunteer action and the interplay of perceptions of the different family generations, the child's prosociality, measured with the child's self-report (and we remind the reader that prosociality is considered one of the strongest determinants in volunteering), was compared to variables such as communication and support in the relationship with offspring (mothers' and fathers' perceptions) and parents' prosociality (fathers' and mothers' perceptions). Analysis showed that the child's prosociality is predicted by the father's support and prosociality; the mother's variables are not determinants and this is true of both volunteers and non-volunteers (Figure 4.5).

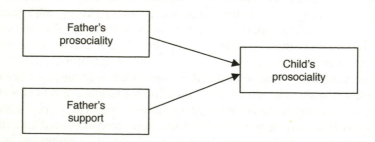

Figure 4.5 Child's prosociality determinants.

In brief . . .

- Families of volunteers do not differ from other families in terms of the quality of the parent–child relationship.
- Mothers and fathers assume different roles in promoting prosocial behaviour: the former offers a concrete example, the latter determines a family climate that promotes commitment.
- The family relations of volunteers reveal internal segmentation: although the majority of volunteers exhibit good, fruitful family relations, volunteers are not without those who experience difficult or very negative relations, once again with the differentiation of mother's and father's role, even if this is a very small percentage of the group.

Conclusions

The scientific literature has attributed to volunteers the status not only of a group, but of a group characterized by high entitativity (Campbell, 1958), meaning by this term the degree with which a social aggregate is perceived by observers to be a unity distinguished by consistency, organization and internal coherence. Specifically, the entitativity of the volunteers' group rests on shared individual and family characteristics that would seem to be distinctive with respect to the outside world, represented by non-volunteers. The findings of our research demonstrate that volunteers are an internally highly heterogeneous group, that their supposed entitativity certainly does not reside in any resemblance of family histories and relations or in the fact of being constituted by altruistic and self-assured individuals, even though they share a common choice to become involved in the social realm. Beyond the stereotypical vision offered by the literature, therefore, volunteers are far from being an internally highly homogeneous and undifferentiated group. On the contrary, we found three groups that are very different from each other due to different characteristics. The cluster, "conscious volunteers—modern donors", and the cluster, "volunteers by chance—needing to belong", incarnate quite faithfully the two prototypical representations of young volunteers tracked and described by studies on the representations of volunteerism (Foster & Fernandes, 1996). First, there is the representation of the young person from a good family, animated by clear, prosocial motivations but well aware of the direct and indirect personal benefits of such an activity; on the other hand, there is the young "religious" person who diverts part of his or her time to volunteer activity, without this being a choice supported by a developed prosociality. This tells us that there is no one typical personality or description of young volunteers, but that, on the contrary, different types of young volunteers coexist, who have diversified traits and characteristics for the most part and that the

motivational differences observed have underlying diversified family relations. In particular, it was seen that wherever family relations are perceived
as being "warm", permeated by support and openness (cluster, "conscious
volunteers"), prosociality had time and space to develop, starting with the
interiorization of the "sense" of one's own family relations that pervades the
capacity of the young person to feel empathy and to dedicate him- or herself
to others. It is probable that parental couples with high congruity in
relational styles towards offspring (adequate, supportive, communicative)
are "rich" families that have known how to give their children hope and a
sense of justice (Cigoli, 1997) and have made them able to open themselves
to the world with confidence in order to give back to others the abundant
gifts that they have received in a sort of "generalized" (Sahlins, 1972) and
"deferred" (Scabini, 1995; Scabini & Cigoli, 2000) reciprocity. We are
dealing with the fascinating hypothesis of the "modern gift" (Godbout,
1992) that is founded on the wish to give back that which one is conscious of
having received from one's own family. Volunteerism then becomes a resti-
tution "to strangers", but finds its specific context in a group that is very
similar to a family, characterized by primary relationships and, as Polanyi
(1974) has said, by exchanges based on reciprocity. The young person
develops motivations for his or her action that clearly have to do with
"conscious prosociality" in which he or she has elaborated not only the
sense but also the benefits of the experience that he or she has chosen to
become involved in. In this way, "doing good" also does the young person
good (Moscovici, 1994), supporting self-esteem and reducing elements of
emotional uncertainty in a generative process for him- or herself and for
others. On the other hand, young people who grow up in a conflicted family
climate (especially when determined by problematical relationships with
mothers), one that is not supportive and is oriented towards disengaged
child-rearing (cluster, "volunteers by chance") invest the volunteer
experience—which is often occasional and limited—with expectations of
improvement strongly directed towards a rather fragile self. Alternatively,
they see in volunteerism a means to express values and community involvement that exclude the desire to help others. This family is a difficult fit
between a mother who completely loses her feminine essence—maternal and
caring—to incarnate a rigidly normative, paternal model and a father whose
only trait is absence: a parental couple, therefore, that does not offer loving
support to the young person, doesn't help him or her to have a sense of self-
confidence, and doesn't allow the young person to see him- or herself as
deserving to be loved.

This young person can neither return nor "give again": prosociality is
consequently lacking or not recognized because, we can hypothesize, it rests
on "altruism without the other" (Moscovici, 1994) or, in other words, on
altruism in which the other is undifferentiated from the self. The helping
relationship in these cases derives from mechanisms of identification and
projection that protect one from the pain of looking inside and seeing the

absence of sure family reference points. Voluntary commitment is born, therefore, perhaps more from the desire/need to find outside what one has not received inside from one's family, with a clear compensatory/reparatory function. The focus is thus not on the person in need of help, the service to offer—often on an irregular basis and for limited hours—but constant affiliation with a group seen as a "substitute" for the family and able to provide the young person with elements of self-identification otherwise not found. We are dealing with prosociality that has been "suggested" by external reference figures, or else that is indirect, incidental, not sought out but adopted as the accepted behaviour of the group itself. Finally, the cluster "volunteers by choice" presents a very interesting relational picture. At first glance, it would seem to be the situation of the greatest relational criticality. The young person perceives a parental couple in which the father—perhaps uncomfortable (high problems in communication and high conflict), little supportive, but "present" at least from a child-rearing point of view—incarnates a traditional, normative role in the absence, however, of a mother with an equally traditional, supportive, and caring role. This mother appears colourless, imitating her husband's relational style in a subdued manner without distinguishing herself in any way and making him appear all the more dominant. These families are marked by the poverty of their bonds, their resources, and their social, economic, and cultural background. The children appear to be unsure of themselves and of their value, but still are able to "give" to others as if, contrary to the research findings, self-esteem and prosociality do not increase one with the other. We can hypothesize that the reasons for the fragility observed in these young people are to be found in part in the difficulty of finding a way to differentiate themselves and their own way of moving outside the family. Engaging in volunteerism can thus assume a function between instrumental—moving out of a poor social environment, doing things and finding possibilities for better activities—and expressive—the desire to do one's best to improve oneself, distinguish oneself, realize aspirations, and express capacities not otherwise visible. Volunteerism thus becomes a space outside the family, but a protected one, in which the young person has the potential to make a "quality jump", experiment, and learn what his or her family was not able to give, and to gain protection from the psychosocial risk.

In contrast to the findings reported in the literature, our research did not reveal differences with respect to the quality of parent–child relations present in the families of volunteers and in families of non-volunteers. The difference is located on the plane of commitment and values, instead. The image that these data reflect back to us of volunteers' families is one in which both parents offer themselves as models for their children, providing not only an adult figure "to imitate" but also multiple opportunities for their children to come into contact with the context of voluntary involvement and helping them, by means of the values they carry and the openness to the social world to which they bear witness, to see the sense of voluntary action and, more in general, of community involvement. While mothers appear to be the ones who provide the concrete models of caring for others in the community, fathers, less materially involved than mothers, are the "invisible register" able to promote the social awakening of their children. Fathers not only offer an alternative to the function of mirroring that mothers exercise for their children, but also support the analysis of and constant check on reality; they inspire confidence and incentivate the acquisition of social skills, thus promoting autonomy, separation, and entry as protagonists into the community. From this a new image of the father emerges, which integrates and condenses the old figure of the father as representative and defender of the law (Lacan, 1977), as dispenser of justice (Cigoli, 1997; Scabini & Cigoli, 2000), and the more recent figure of the father: "empathetic, supportive", conferring sense, accompanying, in his own way, the labyrinth of his child's growth (Pietropolli Charmet, 2000; Shulman & Seiffge-Krenke, 1997). This image of the father and his new function within the family confirm that which has been termed "a values oriented and moral approach to paternity" (Doherty et al., 1998; Hawkins & Dollahite, 1997; Marsiglio, Amato, Day, & Lamb, 2000). This approach is essentially based on the conception of paternity as "generative work" (Erikson, 1982; McAdams & de St Aubin, 1992; Shulman & Seiffge-Krenke, 1997; Snarey, 1993). By "generative work" we mean the attempt to transmit a sense of social responsibility, the capacity to respond to offspring's needs and to help them understand others' needs, support and encouragement towards openness to the social world and ethical and moral commitment to it (Dollahite, Slife, & Hawkins, 1998). The generative father is one who contributes to exchange between the generations and continuously renews it by means of the care he provides as a biological father, as a parent, and as a social father (Snarey, 1993).

FAMILY RELATIONS AND FUTURE EXPECTATIONS

Defining future life plans is unanimously considered to be a developmental task appropriate to adolescence. Adolescents are asked to make choices that involve imagining themselves as future adults: the attainment of educational goals, the acquisition of a professional identity, and the formation of a family could be seen as the most important evidence of having achieved adult status. In other words, future orientation is a developmental task whose pursuit facilitates the transition to adulthood (Seginer, 1995). This task has become even more complex because, as we have mentioned several times, the transition to adulthood as it occurs in complex Western societies has become fragmented into a variety of tracks from which to choose. These retain a minimum of ritual and are characterized by ample space for choice and decision-making concerning the particular mode and timing of the transition (Cigoli, 1995; Scabini, 1995). This fragmentation of the transition to adulthood, connected as it is to the diffusion of growth strategies based on "trial and error", on taking "small steps" at a time or on just waiting (Heinz, 1996)—in other words, the spread of the so-called "paradigm of reversibility" (Ricolfi, 1984)—makes it extremely difficult for present-day younger generations to plan for their futures. This paradigm points to a belief among the younger generation of being able to extend to infinity the possibility of choosing. This belief leads them to construct the present within a plurality of spheres (family, school, work, friendship networks) without the precise coordinates and hierarchies of aims that would presuppose the definition of a unitary value context and general referential systems. A corollary of this paradigm is the "experimentation model", that is, the tendency to make choices "that aren't for life", thus always leaving open the possibility of rethinking choices and modifying them in any area of life: work, the affective realm, friendships. Life has been transformed into a complex succession of situations perceived by young people as being transitory and needing to be selected and organized. Young people, therefore, have many more opportunities but, at the same time, may feel confused and plagued by doubts. The task they must face is not at all simple: they are required to conceive of themselves as being "a planning agency for life's decisions" (Heinz, 1996) and to direct their present and future lives. As Ulrich Beck (1986) has underlined, the situation of transition demands flexibility and a sense of self-direction but, at the same time, requires long-term aspirations together with a certain persistency. To successfully bring about the transition, therefore, young people must be able to quickly and capably select from among immediate options while simultaneously keeping their sights fixed on goals that, given the present organization of society, can only be realized in what seems like a very distant future. The family affects young people's future planning in different ways: by mediating the influence of the social context but also by directly proposing models and values and making explicit its expectations for the young person's future. A less direct type of influence exists, moreover, which acts through the quality of family relationships. But while there is a consistent body of research pointing to social influence on young people's expectations, only a few studies have focused on the influence exercised by family context on the younger generation's future planning. In the following section, we will detail the findings of our studies on future orientation and those having to do with parents' and children's expectations about the domains of work and study.

Late adolescents' expectations about school and work

The theme of expectations highlights more than any other the reciprocal relationship between individual, family, and society. Indeed, individual projects are influenced by a host of economic, social, and cultural factors: in short, they are determined by the social structure that Lewin (1946) had already identified as the fundamental element of a total temporal prospect. The influence of these two factors acts directly on the late adolescent by means of the representation that he or she has constructed over years spent in the social environment but is also mediated by individual factors (interests, self-esteem levels, values, etc.) and family factors (parents' child-rearing style, levels of aspirations, family history, relationships). As a matter of fact, norms, values, and models that influence young people's future planning are transmitted from one generation to the next in the family. Moreover, parents bear the fundamental task of guiding young people with respect to future choices and providing direction to their child's growth (Scabini, 1995). Working out plans for the future is thus a developmental task that involves the entire family unit, in that it takes place within the network of family relationships. Research examining young people's expectations has first of all pointed to the existence of gender differences imputable to the effects of the process of sexual role socialization: this is the process by which individuals learn which behaviours the social context defines as being appropriate to one's gender. In particular, research has focused on academic and professional expectations in young people: this has been a favourite area of investigation into the causal antecedents of occupational segregation in the work place, due to which women are employed in typically feminine sectors and tend to occupy lower levels on the hierarchical ladder. Different studies (Manganelli Rattazzi & Capozza, 1993; Rosen & Aneshensel, 1978; Sandberg, Ehrhardt, Ince, & Meyer-Bahlburg, 1991) have revealed that young people's expectations faithfully reproduce the same differences existing in the world of work, in the sense that girls plan for a shorter academic career and aspire to lower professional levels: it seems that the awareness of the difficulty of reconciling family and work leads to a lowering of girls' investment in areas of school and work. The same differences were found in the expectations that parents nurture for the academic and professional futures of their children, thus confirming the crucial role played by the family in the process of sexual role socialization (Manganelli Rattazzi & Capozza, 1993; Rosen & Aneshensel, 1978).

Late adolescents' expectations: differences due to gender and socioeconomic status

In terms of academic expectations, our studies (database B. FRAP, 1994 [see Appendix, Table 1] age range 16–19 years) show that, overall, late adolescents have rather high expectations for their academic careers, and that this is true above all for girls. In terms of their professional expectations, a certain number of late adolescents reveal *uncertainty in predicting their working future*. Those who are able to identify a profession hypothesize prestigious, high-level careers. Only 1.2% of girls plan to be housewives, a far lower percentage than that of mothers who carry out unpaid work in the home. Therefore, almost all the girls plan to work outside the home. Professional expectations differ according to the late adolescent's gender: girls aspire to high-level professions, in keeping with their very high academic aspirations, while boys, more than girls, aspire to low-level professions.

Late adolescents' academic plans are closely tied to their family's economic resources and social standing. It was found that young people from families with a low socioeconomic status are more inclined than their peers to aspire to diplomas from secondary or technical-vocational schools and less likely to aspire to a university education. Late adolescents from middle-class families are more likely than their peers to aspire to obtaining only a secondary school diploma, while young people from upper-class families, who hold the secondary school diploma in low regard, plan to obtain a university degree. Expectations about work are also influenced by the family's status. Late adolescents of a lower socioeconomic status foresee working in lower-level jobs. No significant interaction emerged between the middle status and late adolescents' expectations about work: evidently various possibilities present themselves to these young people. The children of upper-class families—as expected—have high occupational aspirations. An analysis of the measures of association between the variables examined revealed that both academic and professional expectations depend to a greater degree on the family's socioeconomic level than on the late adolescent's gender. We feel it is also important to note that when socioeconomic status is equal, the late adolescent's gender influences work expectations more than academic expectations. This indicates that the former are more subject to gender stereotyping than the latter.

Parents' expectations for their children's future

Let us now turn to the expectations parents nurture for their children's academic careers. Parents have rather high aspirations for their offspring in this area. Parents have differentiated expectations for their children according to gender: mothers, in particular, contrary to what one might think, envision daughters, more than sons, obtaining a university degree. Furthermore, it emerged that parents in families of low socioeconomic standing, more than others, think it more probable that their offspring will complete their secondary school education, while believing it quite improbable that they would attend university or complete a postgraduate degree. For middle-class families, all levels of instruction are equally probable. Parents at the highest socioeconomic level have aspirations that see their children obtaining a university or postgraduate degree and believe it improbable that they would stop after completing secondary school.

Families' socioeconomic status influences parents' academic plans for their offspring more than the latter's gender, echoing the findings for late adolescents' academic expectations. Let us now review the analysis of parents' expectations for their children's future working lives. In general, parents have rather high expectations for offspring's careers: only a minimal percentage, around 1%, believe their daughters will work only in the home. Parents predict professional paths that differ according to a child's gender: both parents believe that daughters, more than sons, will achieve a professional level classified as "low-highest". Mothers, moreover, think sons more than daughters will reach a "high-lowest" occupational level while daughters will reach a "low-medium" level. In formulating their expectations for their children's professional futures, parents keep in mind their own family's socioeconomic level. In fact, the expectations of mothers and fathers of low social standing gravitate towards "high-lowest" and "high-medium" occupational levels, and rarely towards the highest level. The responses from middle-class parents, however, are distributed equally over all levels. Upper-class fathers and mothers expect that one day their children will engage in high-level professions and think it improbable that they will work in middle-level occupations. The fathers of this social class also provide the answer "I don't know" with a greater probability than can be attributed to chance.

A comparison of parents and children

To test for agreement between parents and offspring, we constructed a discrepancy index between the expectations of parents and those of offspring (see Chapter 2). The use of this index revealed that, except in a very few cases, parents and children are in perfect agreement about the latter's academic and professional futures. As far as academic expectations are concerned, no differences were found between sons and daughters in relation to the discrepancy index with mothers. A significant difference was found, however, with respect to the discrepancy between fathers and sons, in the sense that the discrepancy between them is decidedly higher than that between fathers and daughters. No differences were found in occupational expectations, however. If one compares late adolescents' plans with those of parents, greater agreement[12] is found between sons and mothers than sons and fathers, and this agreement is greater than that between parents and daughters, as compared to sons.

To evaluate the family's influence on late adolescents' expectations, we used a causal model (path analysis) created according to the specifications of Rosen and Aneshensel (1978), who hypothesize that late adolescents' academic and professional expectations are explained by a set of variables such as socioeconomic status, parents' level of instruction, number of family members, a child's academic success, mothers' and fathers' expectations, and self-esteem. If we consider data relating to the influence of parents' expectations on the formative plans of sons, the first finding that emerges from a summary glance at the data has to do with mothers' role: maternal expectations constitute the variable that more than any other explains late adolescents' plans.

The data analysis (Figure 4.6) also reveals that fathers do not influence their sons directly by means of their expectations but only by their professional level, an indicator of the family unit's social status as well as available economic resources. It must be highlighted, however, that fathers influence their sons' expectations through the mothers' expectations, which are significantly correlated with those of their spouses. One might say that mothers become the interpreters and spokespersons for fathers' desires for their sons.

Mothers' educational levels influence the plans of both parents. When thinking about a son's future, parents also take into account the child's academic success, a variable that therefore has only an indirect effect on sons' plans. Self-esteem does not seem to be connected in any way to sons' expectations. The results on daughters' academic expectations are very different. Girls, in fact, when formulating future plans, take into account the desires of both fathers and mothers, even if the mothers' wishes carry considerably more weight than those of fathers. Mothers, moreover, also act as role models, since they influence their daughters through their educational level.

The other fundamental discrepancy with the model relating to sons has to do with the role played by academic success. Indeed, in the case of boys, this variable had only an indirect effect, acting through parents' expectations. Parents also keep this variable in mind when thinking about the future formative path their daughters will take. Self-esteem, furthermore, plays a crucial role for girls, a factor that was completely absent in the case of boys. The father's educational level seems to influence both parents' expectations. A comparison of the findings for boys and girls leads us to conclude that sons' expectations are determined above all by maternal aspirations and by the family's socioeconomic status, whereas those of daughters are first determined by maternal expectations and second by paternal expectations, as well as by self-esteem and the assessment they receive from teachers.

Turning to expectations about work, the most significant finding to have emerged from the data analysis for boys has to do once again with the mothers' role. Mothers' expectations are the only variable that directly influences boys' plans. Given that fathers' expectations are strongly correlated with those of mothers, we could hypothesize, as we did in the case of educational expectations, that mothers act as interpreters of fathers' aspirations for their sons. Both parents, moreover, use the father's professional level as a reference point in formulating plans for their son. This variable, therefore, has only an indirect effect on the son's aspirations, mediated by maternal expectations. Girls as well, when thinking about their future professional life, allow themselves to be influenced mainly by their mothers' expectations.

The variable, "mother's occupational expectations" influences, more than any other, the dependent variable in both the subsample of boys and in that of girls.

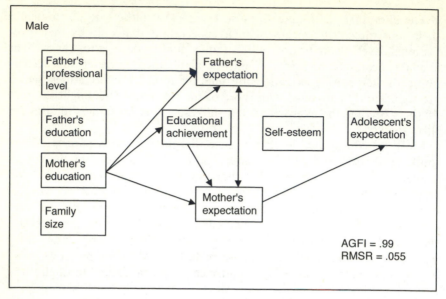

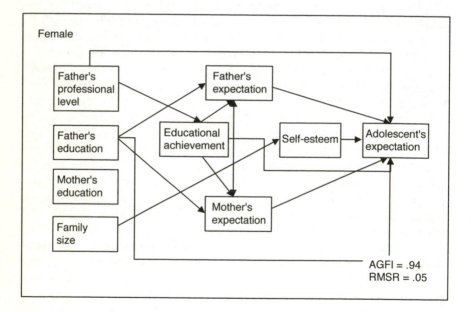

Figure 4.6 Influence of parent's expectation on adolescent academic expectation by gender.

Conclusions

We may conclude, then, that mothers guide their children's professional choices in the case of both sons and daughters. Fathers' aspirations turn out to be highly correlated with those of mothers and do not significantly differ from these. Thus, it seems that mothers act as spokespersons with their children in communicating the desires of both parents for their sons' and daughters' futures. Mothers, moreover, function as the principal agents for the socialization of children in terms of gender roles in the family, directing sons and daughters towards differentiated paths.

That mothers play the central role in family relations is a finding that has by now been confirmed by a great many studies (Greene & Grimsley, 1990; Miller & Lane, 1991; Youniss & Ketterlinus, 1987); however, that mothers function in transmitting norms, values, and models that have to do with the social sphere, traditionally considered to be the domain of fathers, appears to be new. To summarize, mothers influence the academic and work choices of their children (both male and female) and also convey the father's expectations for his children (Rosnati, 1995). If we consider the first model, regarding the family's influence on children's cultural plans, the most surprising feature of all is the mother's role, in that she exerts a predominant influence on male aspirations. Fathers serve as models for sons in terms of their professional achievement, but not directly in terms of parental expectations, although the strong correlation between fathers' and mothers' expectations should also be noted. By contrast, daughters take both parents into account, although the mother's direct influence is greater than that of the father because she influences her daughter's educational plans by means of her expectations and educational level.

Thus, even tasks traditionally assigned to fathers, such as guidance in the choice of work or career, are being performed by mothers in Italian families with late adolescents.

Future orientation: a comparison of late adolescents' and their parents' views

In this section we present the data from our research related to late adolescents' future orientation and parents' expectations for their children. Due to the nature of constructs being discussed and, in order to avoid redundancy in the presentation of the data, we have decided in this case to directly set forth the comparison between generations. With this aim in mind, drawing on database G. AFOFA, 2000 (see Appendix, Table 1), we first investigated the number of hopes and fears and the thematic differentiation index, that is, the number of domains quoted by late adolescents and parents. The analysis of the mean scores demonstrates that both generations have an optimistic vision of the future: the mean number of hopes quoted is greater than that of fears. A comparison of the two generations revealed

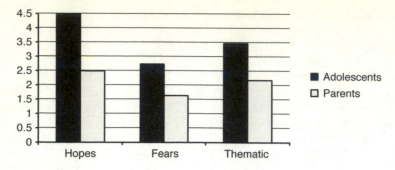

Figure 4.7 Adolescents' and parents' hopes, fears and thematic differentiation
index.

that the late adolescents quoted a greater number of both hopes and fears
than their parents. The mean of the thematic differentiation index revealed
that late adolescents, when thinking about their futures, consider a greater
number of life domains than their parents do (Figure 4.7). In other words,
when imagining their children's future, parents "anchor" it to a limited
number of domains, whereas the younger generations display a more com-
posite and complex vision of the domains constituting their future lives. In
addition, while parents list hopes and fears regarding only the life domains
connected to a normative transition to the adult world (school, work,
family, success), their children, in accordance with other research (Nurmi,
1987, 1989a, 1989b; Seginer, 1988a, 1988b), consider other areas less clearly
linked to a stereotypical transition. Thus, this first result indicates that late
adolescents have more articulated and complex views of their own futures
and are increasingly attentive to more life areas than their parents are.
Nevertheless, both the late adolescents and their parents most often mentioned expectations related to future work, future family, education, and
general success. These results confirm the findings of numerous studies
carried out on late adolescents' future orientation. Our data reveal, however, that not only do late adolescents express expectations more closely
related to the perspective of the life course but that parents share the same
perspective. For each of the three domains most frequently chosen (school,
work, future family) we probed the relationship between the quality of
communication and levels of control and optimism expressed by late adolescents. Our research found no significant differences for communication
with parents in the case of sons. For daughters, communication with fathers
was found to be the significant factor for the level of realization in the work
domain and the level of control in the family domain. In particular,
daughters who report better communication with their fathers have a higher
level of optimism with respect to their professional aspirations than girls
who perceive worse communication. As for the family domain, girls who
report good communication with their fathers have more internalized levels

of control than their peers. Perceptions regarding communication with mothers are a significant factor for control levels and the probability of realization in the school domain. In particular, girls who report above average communication with their mothers were found to have more internally located control and higher levels of optimism than daughters who perceive worse communication. These general results allow us to identify two different profiles in relation to late adolescents' gender. The girls predict that they will finish their studies and enter the work force sooner than their parents think likely, both being events that they believe themselves able to control to a greater extent than parents believe possible (with the exception of the school domain, for which they have the same perceptions as their fathers). Furthermore, they share perceptions with their parents as to the age at which they will realize the goal of starting a family and the possibility of controlling this event, but are decidedly more pessimistic as far as the realization of all these goals is concerned (with the exception of the realization of academic plans, for which they shared their mothers' perceptions). The boys, for their part, predict that they will finish their studies sooner than their parents expect and differ only from their fathers in predicting when they will start a family, while they agree with both parents on when they will enter the work force. They give evidence of a more internally situated locus of control and greater pessimism than their parents do as to the possibility of realizing school and work goals (with the exception of the possibility of realizing future work plans, where mothers and sons were found to have the same perceptions); they share with parents the type of control they feel able to exert and the possibility of realization in the family domain.

Conclusions

Parents and offspring from Italian families share the latter's positive vision of the future, characterized more by optimism than by fear. The comparison between the generations allowed us to highlight the differing degrees of involvement on the part of parents and children in planning the younger generation's future. In fact, while it was very clear that the generations shared a hopeful vision of adult life, it should be noted that younger generations expressed their hopes with greater incisiveness. This discrepancy between parents and children is amplified when the analytical unit becomes the family dyad and with the relative degree of internal harmony between the generations. There are some areas that were chosen in common: work, school, family, and health. These areas once again essentially involve adult life and demonstrate the importance the transition to adult status assumes for both generations. The data show that the choice of work unites the greatest number of family dyads, indicating the centrality of this domain in both generations' future perspectives. If, on the one hand, parents and children confirm the hypothesis that a "cultural prototype" exists regarding future orientation (Nurmi, 1991), in that they agree on the order of the various normative steps involved in future planning (finishing one's education, entering the work force, building a family) and locate the realization of these goals between the second and third decade of life, they nevertheless differ as to temporal extension, control beliefs, and the possibility that the children's goals can be achieved. Young people and parents seem to have two different approaches. The young people believe themselves to be able to reach their goals and to be able to do so sooner than their parents think possible and yet, at the same time, they believe they are less likely to fulfil their aspirations. This result suggests two interpretations. On the one hand, this relative "pessimism" during the transition to adulthood could testify to a certain realism in the youngsters who, although seeing themselves as being competent, do not deny the objective difficulties of finding work today or finishing a course of study. On the other hand, it could attest to a certain "fragility" in late adolescents, attributable either to the fear of "failing" or to the need to better understand how to manage their abilities and competencies in a world that inspires apprehension. Parents, for their part, have less faith in their children's opportunities but express greater optimism in their assessment of the probability of achieving goals. The overall analysis of these findings paints a surprising picture, which differs from the results obtained by earlier studies: we find that there is greater agreement in perceptions regarding the variables, not between mothers and daughters, but between mothers and sons, especially with respect to the two domains most closely connected to the transition to adulthood, family and work. This also extends to the age and possibility of realization. Another consideration having to do with temporal extension, control belief, and the possibility of realizing set goals is that the perceptual agreement between daughters and parents concerns the family and school domains while differences were found only with respect to the work domain. In the case of sons, on the other hand, there was perceptual sharing with respect to the domains of work and family, while differences were found in the area of school. This result implies that while starting a family is a domain shared by the two generations both as an objective to be reached and in terms of means and age, irrespective of the child's gender, in the case of school and work several differences linked to gender emerge (Lanz, Rosnati, Marta, & Scabini, 2001). It seems that daughters experience within the family a situation of greater perceptive divergence from their mothers than their male peers, and yet mothers are traditionally described as being their preferred confidantes. Bearing in mind that in Italy the entry of women into the work force in great numbers, and the equal treatment of sons and daughters in terms of professional prospects are recent phenomena, we believe that the perceptual divergence found between girls and their mothers regarding the work domain are a clear indicator of the social changes under way in our country. Although mothers and daughters prioritize the choice of work in the daughters' future plans, they show substantial differences regarding the means to adopt in order to fulfil this goal. The generation of mothers seems to counterbalance that of their daughters: indeed, while the latter, as we have seen, predict an earlier entry into the working world, they see themselves as bearing more responsibility in realizing this event, and imagine it in essentially pessimistic terms. The mothers, less naïve, more realistic, and more aware of social ties and economic contingencies, predict that their daughters will commence work at a later age, are more apt to take into consideration the possible influence that situational factors can have on realizing this goal, and show greater optimism. The importance of the relationship between daughters and mothers in this area is testified to by the influence that communication quality with this parent exercises on the perceptions that daughters have of personal control with respect to future plans and the possibility of carrying them out. In line with the results of other studies, supportive communication with mothers encourages greater internal control and optimism in daughters. To complete the picture, we should add that, as regards expectations about realizing professional goals, communication with fathers also exerts a positive influence on daughters, which is to say that they are sensitive, as far as our object of analysis is concerned, to the relationship with both parents.

In brief . . .

- Mothers exert great influence on future choices, a task that has been traditionally attributed to fathers.
- There are numerous differences between boys and girls.
- Late adolescents perceive their own future as being very complex and rich in possibilities as compared to their parents, but agree with them about which future developmental domains are most significant: family, work, health.

CONCLUDING REFLECTIONS

In this chapter we have seen once again how the comparison between genders and generations makes it possible to gather valuable and otherwise inaccessible information regarding both the condition of psychosocial risk during the transition to adulthood and young people's families' planning process for the future. In particular, the research discussed in these pages makes an important contribution to the understanding of fathers' and mothers' roles in determining the different outcomes in question—the condition of psychosocial risk in late adolescence and young adulthood, the espousal of prosocial behaviour, and planning for the future.

Concluding remarks and new research questions

We began this work with a presentation of our fundamental theoretical perspective. This was not by chance but reflected a long-pondered choice that originated in a simple consideration: much of the literature on the family relations of late adolescents and young adults seems to investigate micro-questions, sometimes with excellent methodological virtuoso performances, but without defining the research object in a precise manner, without stating which theory is being referred to, and, as a consequence, reaching precise but limited micro-results. Indeed, it is difficult in these cases to furnish broader interpretations and meanings. The relational–intergenerational perspective proposed here incorporates in itself contributions from other theories and perspectives having to do with family relations and acts both as a link in the chain and a comparison between them. As has been suggested by Abrams and Hogg (2004):

> It certainly helps to have a metatheory tucked away in one's backpack. A metatheory is like a good travel guide—it tells you where to go and where not to go, what is worthwhile and what is not, the best way to get to a destination, and where it is best to rest a while. Metatheoretical conviction provides structure and direction, it informs the sorts of questions one asks and does not ask, and it furnishes a passion that makes the quest exciting and buffers one from disappointments along the way.
>
> (Abrams & Hogg, 2004, p. 98)

The relational–intergenerational perspective has functioned for us as a compass, guiding and orienting our research on family relations, providing us with clear input for the consequent research methodology, legitimizing various research-related questions and statistical procedures, and revisiting others where they proved to be unsatisfactory. When considering the family as the organization that is located at the intersecting point of gender and generational lines, this perspective makes it possible to gather global data for the whole system, but also prevents us from losing either individual or dyadic data. In other words, it enables us to see the forest and the trees, the big picture and the details, and the connections between the details, considered in terms of gender and generation."Kurt Lewin's dictum, that there is nothing more practical than a good theory, applies not only to designing our social world, but also to discovering it" (Trope, 2004, p. 199): in our opinion, the relational-intergenerational perspective fully respects Lewin's dictum. Its application over the 15-year span of our research on family relations in families that are facing their children's transition to adulthood allows us to proffer considerations and reflections on what has been done and on future developments, in terms of both theory and methodology.

WHICH VARIABLES FOR FAMILY STUDY?

The analysis of the research findings presented here in the light of the relational–intergenerational perspective suggests at least two considerations. The research presented has enabled us to detect some constant trends in the functioning of families of late adolescents and young adults. Faced with a very positive assessment of family relations expressed by both generations and both genders, we were able to discern substantial and significant differences between genders and generations by means of a closer and more precise analysis. In the first place, parents reveal a more positive and kinder vision of family relations in terms of support, communication, and satisfaction than that expressed by their children. The latter seem to be more realistic in evaluating family relations, making distinctions with respect to a parent's gender and exhibiting differentiated relational modalities with respect to their own gender as well. Indeed, mothers are held to be the more supportive parent by both sons and daughters, the one with whom one communicates the most and with the most ease. But, beyond this general finding, in family relations we seem to see perceptive convergences and true alliances defined by gender. In fact, if we consider communication, we discover that boys claim to experience less difficulty with fathers as compared to girls, and that the latter claim to experience less difficulty with mothers as compared to boys. Thus, as regards family satisfaction, the males of both generations, fathers and sons, show higher scores than the females in the family, mothers and daughters. The latter finding is easily understood if we think about the transformations in the female role that have occurred over the past 20 years and about the different psychology of gender. As a matter of fact, for mothers, the recent sociodemographic and role-related changes that have come to pass in modern societies have led the woman to increasingly assume a central role in family relations, to overburden herself in terms of children's upbringing and guidance, and to dedicate herself to managing the delicate balance between the duties of family and work. When it comes to daughters, they show a more sophisticated and detailed reading of reality than boys do, and seem to have greater need of relational coherence than them. Girls, there-fore, are more sensible of discrepancies and incoherence that do not emerge from a superficial reading of reality. This perceptive sharing and probably a pronounced "mirroring" of mothers in their daughters give rise to a strong "feminine alliance", that is, between mothers and daughters with respect to the latter's work choices. As a matter of fact, aside from the objective problems that could interpose themselves between the wish and the goal, mothers and daughters aim for high-level educational and employment objectives, with a utopian belief that they are "perfectly" reconcilable with "having a family". An important finding of our research is the centrality of the father's role in determining his child's psychosocial risk. We have observed a perceptive agreement between fathers and their late adolescent offspring, specifically with regard to the problematic and negative aspects in their mutual relationships. Mothers, on the contrary, seem to be afflicted with a sort of blindness in the sense of being unable or of finding it impossible to accurately perceive the quality of their relationships with their children. To this should be added that in satisfied families the relational imbalance towards the mother, typical of Italian families, is "corrected" by the father's making himself available to assist his child in choices regarding future work and/or study. In this way, he contributes to the children's drive towards individual and social self-fulfilment. Moreover, our research on young volunteers and their parents has shown us that mothers have a central role in determining a child's involvement in volunteerism but that this influence has deeper roots in the attitude and prosocial behaviour of fathers. The father is a model to imitate: he provides sense and meaning; he promotes his child's birth into society and his/her entry into the social community by facilitating autonomy, trust in society, separation through the analysis of reality and the drive to acquire social skills. In other words, it seems that the fathers in our samples are able to enact generative fathering: as Marsiglio et al. (2000, 1177), in accordance with Snarey (1993) and Dollahite and Hawkins (1998), recently remarked, 'The generative work of fathers involves a sense of responsible caring, a desire to facilitate the needs of the next generation, and attention to fostering a fit between men's activities and children's needs'. In brief, in the Italian context, therefore, the parental couple with late adolescent/young adult children is characterized by a schism between parents: father perceives a child's difficulties and those of the relationship with him or her, but he is powerless to act; mother is blind to this difficulty and continues to behave as if all is well in the relationship. On the other hand, the data from our research highlight the fact that young people today do not have significant adult figures who can offer points of reference outside the family. In practical terms, these data on late adolescents and their parents can be translated into proposals for intervention aimed at supporting families in the difficult transition to adulthood. Faced with a social context that pushes young adults to the "margins", and composed of families that seem to want to protect them at all costs, it is necessary to promote interventions that put young people in the centre, allowing them to measure themselves with other adults and peers and to establish significant relationships. We are speaking of organizing support groups, focused especially on the quality of dyadic relationships and led by an expert, with the ability to make connections and distinctions between people and bonds. In particular, priority during this work should be given to the dyadic relationships with friends and with partners, aspects and topics that are difficult to share in the family. The transition to adulthood, as amply discussed in Chapter 1, cannot be considered a solitary journey but involves the whole family. For this reason, parents must also be included in interventions with the goal of understanding their difficulty in allowing their child to leave home, of raising the quality of communicative exchanges and improving support for the adolescent child. In this case, as well, the work must focus on the dyadic relationship with the child, knowing how to use fathers' perceptive accuracy with respect to the relationship with offspring, not only to glean reliable information but also to help mothers face up to their own "perceptive blindness". This finding suggests that, in the Italian context, even though mothers play a pivotal role in family functioning, we must take into account fathers' perspective in order to have at our disposal an accurate picture of the adolescent's situation. These data demand that the father's role and function in the Italian family be taken into greater consideration by psychosocial practitioners. Extraneous to the scope of the present work is further exploration of the topic of techniques applicable to work in groups aimed at adolescents and parents. Closely connected, however, is a concerted effort to think, and then act, in terms of the research results in order to identify specific forms of support to direct at both children and their parents, with the goal of opposing the slippage of situations of psychosocial risk towards relational pathology. These forms of support of the transition to adulthood (Coleman & Karraker, 1998) can be inserted into specifically designed programmes or into a broader treatment plan that constitutes the relaunching and revitalization of family bonds and, more particularly, of the parent–child relationship. In our opinion, the second option allows for obtaining more efficacious and long-lasting results because the intervention is aimed not only at facilitating the acquisition of skills and abilities but also, and above all, at empowering and regenerating bonds, while also safeguarding symbolic aspects. Side by side, or synergistically, with interventions that see the family as playing the role of protagonist, interventions may also be orchestrated that give the protagonist's role to other social actors from the community in which the family lives: for example, the school or university and organizations for leisure time and social involvement. Especially in cases where parents have difficulty doing full justice to their child-rearing role, these institutions can also carry out an important "social" function with respect to late adolescents and young adults by preventing or limiting deviant and antisocial behaviours. In equal measure, these institutions can bolster up the family in understanding, interpreting and managing manifestations of risk and in acting preventively to avoid these being associated with deviant behaviours. In this way, prevention and intervention in the deviant situation become a means of regenerating the social bond (for further discussion of this theme, see Scabini & Iafrate, 2003).

As to the quality of the parent–child relationship and risk, in this work we have presented comparisons between intact biological families and adoptive or broken families. Classically, the literature uses the first group of families or adolescents as the control group with respect to the other two. This type of research has undoubtedly produced useful information but what it denies is the specificity of the challenges and obstacles that diverse families must face and overcome. And here we come to the second consideration: the reader must certainly have noticed the fact that the research data presented herein refer above all to variables of an affective nature— communication, support and satisfaction—while variables of an ethical nature were left in the background. The choice of affective variables is the result of a consideration of the national and international literature in which such constructs occupied the foreground and, indeed, almost the entire stage, leaving in the shadows other variables of a more ethical nature, for example, control. In other words, we feel confident in forwarding the hypothesis that the international research of the past decade, on the tails of a tendency to theorize adolescence as a harmonious and serene transition to adulthood, has colluded with the image of an affective family and has ended up investigating above all those variables that confirm this new vision that stands in contrast to the medicalist view of this period as one of "storm and stress". We have thus witnessed in these years an avalanche of research on support and communication, while such constructs as control and conflict were relegated to the background or, at least, were more frequently investigated in cases of broken or non-biological families. Having established certain results related to satisfaction and, especially, communication and support, these constructs were in part obscured by others that, in the meantime, in a play of light and shadow, ventured out into the bright lights and conquered centre stage after years of neglect because they had acquired a central position in the theoretical discussions of researchers of late adolescents' and young adults' family relations. From a focus on communication, an affective variable, we have moved today to a focus on variables such as monitoring, clearly of ethical origin. It is as if the research on adolescents, after having investigated in depth the affective aspect that was put on display by families with adolescents, after having sounded out what constituted the most dazzling element of the change in parent–child relations during the adolescent phase, now asks itself clear questions about ethical aspects as well. The difficulty in considering ethical variables, however, can be attributed in part to the different course they take compared to affective variables and to the difficulties in measurements and comparisons that this implies. Because, if it is true that communication, support, and satisfaction maintain elements of invariance with reference to offspring's age—openness in communication is always positive, whether at 11 years of age or 15, 19 or 24—ethical variables acquire different meaning and value exactly in relation to age, so much so that some, with the increase in a child's age, lose sense and are substituted by others. For example, monitoring, which is enjoying so much success in recent years, is a variable that—in our opinion, but the international research seems to be moving in the same direction—is sensibly investigated in early or middle adolescence; by late adolescence it reveals itself to be hardly appropriate and it would seem sensible to substitute it with variables such as trust, commitment, or values, that is, variables that demonstrate how much the late adolescent and young adults have interiorized values-related aspects.

It is not by chance, therefore, that in recent years, notwithstanding that it is still considered rather as a "niche" phenomenon in terms of numbers, many studies have been dedicated to the civic engagement of young people and, in particular, to their involvement in the area of volunteerism and to how the family can promote either one or the other (Kirkpatrick-Johnson et al., 1998; Youniss, Bales, Christmas-Best, Diversi, McLaughlin, & Silbereisen, 2003). Our research findings, for example, clearly show that the families of young volunteers do not exhibit "exceptional" traits as to their functioning and the quality of their internal relationships as compared to their non-volunteer peers. We are dealing with "normal" families, from this point of view, who experience the joy and the hardships of everyday life like any other families, facing critical events and moments of happiness just as they do, but distinguish themselves from the others by an element that they share among themselves, that is to say, a particular relational modality with their community and time. These are families that experience the context of belonging with trust and hope, justice and commitment, loyalty and fairness. This appears to constitute a sort of "compass" or motivational push for the children of these families in the difficult journey of growth, today more than ever marked by uncertainties and fear of the future. This example shows us how important the consideration of ethical variables (trust, loyalty, commitment . . .) is if we are to fully understand the family relations of late adolescents and young adults.

WHICH METHODOLOGY FOR WHICH FAMILY?

What we mean by family, and what its peculiarities are, has been amply described elsewhere in this work. How can we capture the essence of the family, understood as the organization that positions itself at the inter-secting point of gender and generational lines, without losing sight of global, dyadic and individual aspects? As we saw in Chapter 2, having several points of view on the relationship seems essential if the researcher is to understand "the family" as a family, rather than as just one person's perspective of that system (Sabatelli & Bartle, 1995). The research presented in the preceding chapters made use of more than one informant and of data analysis techniques that today we would define as being "classic or traditional" (MANOVA, regressions, etc.). In recent years we have seen the rapid diffusion of techniques for data analysis that had made their first timid and sporadic appearance in the 1980s and began to circulate among students of family relations during the transition to adulthood towards the end of the 1990s: we are referring to structural equation models (SEM). Beginning in the 1980s, structural equation modelling began to become prominent in the family literature, thus providing researchers with new instruments for data analysis capable of dealing with just that multiplicity of information that, with the usual techniques, one was forced not to take into account. With SEM, researchers were able to go beyond regression-based path analysis to study both measurement and structural models. Thomson and Williams' (1982) article was among the first to introduce structural models as a tool for dealing with data from multiple informants. The idea that to capture family relations it is necessary to have multiple informants thus began to gain ground in those years. Structural equation modelling constitutes an interesting way to deal with family data in that it forces researchers to think in terms of models and to ask themselves how to connect different points of view. Structural equation modelling affords researchers the opportunity to create a single, latent construct with multiple indicators, accounting for the correlations between indicators and measurement error (Lavee, 1988). Deal (1995), to highlight how to connect the divergent and convergent perspectives in family studies, uses confirmatory factor analysis, bringing this analysis into force on data obtained from father, mother, and two children on the Family Environment Scale (Moos & Moos, 1981). The model tested by Deal estimates two types of latent variable: the common family factor that emerges from the reports of the four family members and four latent variables, one for each family member. In this case, the four latent variables are thought of as uniqueness; they are the variance in each family member's report that is not shared with other family members. While it is true that error variance may indeed be a part of this, the unique perceptions of the individual are also contained in these latent variables. This model is a confirmatory factor analysis in which the variance of the family members' scores is disentangled in what members share (common family factor) and in what is specific to each member (error). This way of analysing data conforms to both convergent and divergent approaches because it allows the researcher to obtain information at both individual and family levels. Moreover, in this analysis, factor scores show each member's "contribution" in determining the common score: in other words, they can be interpreted as gauges of the "reliability level" of each member in assessing a specific family construct. But does a single, latent family variable exist or could we hypothesize the existence of more than one latent factor that would explain variance of families? And should the measures reported by each family member be considered independently of each other, or not? Researchers have responded to these queries by testing models with more than one latent variable and by using the multitrait–multimethod approach proposed by Campbell and Fiske (1959). The application of the multitrait–multimethod approach to family studies allows us to measure several constructs (for example, cohesion in the father–child dyad, in the mother–child dyad, and in the father–mother dyad) with several methods (child's point of view, mother's point of view, father's point of view). This approach makes it possible to define which is the more reliable point of view in the data collected for a specific dyad (convergent validity) and to assess whether dyads are really different from each other (discriminant validity). This approach has been called the multidyadic–multiperspective approach by Cole and Jordan (1989) to indicate that several dyads and several perspectives are considered. For each dyadic relationship, all family members' perspectives are collected, that is to say, each family member is asked to provide responses with regard to each family dyad. A variant of this method is the correlated uniqueness model (Kenny & Kashy, 1992), which requires that each measurement error be correlated with the other measurement errors from the same subject. The correlation between measurement errors of the same subject could be considered as an indicator of the "method" effect. The advantage of this model is that it allows for a better estimation of the "trait" factor (Sabatelli & Bartle, 1995), but the problem is that it is not possible to disentangle the random error and the error due to the "method". When a family latent variable is found, the problem is its interpretation. It is clear that family members have some shared variance that determines the family latent variable, but we don't know whether what doesn't fall into this factor is due to individual differences or to dyadic characteristics (Bartle-Haring, Kenny, & Gavazzi, 1999).

A relational methodology to family study: the Social Relational Model

In this section we introduce a model that allows us to consider the different levels of analysis that characterize family research (individual, dyadic, and family). Moreover, this model makes it possible to manage the non-independence of family data: it explicitly examines the non-independence in social interaction data as a way of studying the reciprocity of social interaction (Kenny & Judd, 1986). This is the Social Relational Model (SRM), originally developed by David Kenny and his colleagues for the analysis of round robin designs (see Kenny & La Voie, 1984), in which data are collected on the behaviour, perceptions, or feelings of each member of a group in relation to each of the other group members. Because each member of a family has a relationship with each of the other family members, data on these relationships conform to a round robin design (Cook, 1994). The applicability of the SRM to the study of family relationships was recognised in the 1980s, and it has subsequently been used in some interesting studies (Branje, van Aken, & van Lieshout, 2002; Cook, 1993, 2000, 2001; Cook & Douglas, 1998; Delsing, Oud, De Bruyn, & van Aken, 2003; van Aken, Oud, Mathijssen, & Koot, 2001). According to the family SRM, the relationship of one family member to another is a function of four systematic sources of variance and of error (Cook, 1994); these five components are independent:

1. Actor effect: a generalized tendency of a family member to see others in a particular way.
2. Partner effect: a generalized tendency of a family member to be seen by others in a similar way.
3. Relationship effect: the unique perception of a family member about his/her relationship with a particular family member, independently of the actor and partner effects.
4. Family effect: about the family characteristics; these characteristics influence the individual perception of family members.
5. Error: what isn't explained by the other effects.

The actor and partner effects represent the individual level, relationship effect is the dyadic level, and family effect is the family level that are present in the perception of relationships (Cook, 1993). An SRM analysis is essentially a confirmatory factor analysis in which the family, actor, partner, and relationship effects are latent variables.

There are 12 observed measures in a two-parent, two-child family; each is specified to be a function of four such components. The family effect is common to all 12 measures, but there are separate actor and partner effects for each role in the family. Thus, one family effect, four actor effects (mother, father, child 1 and child 2), and four partner effects (mother, father, child 1 and child 2) must be specified in the model (Cook, 1994). Within this model, some of these effects may correlate, giving rise to reciprocity indices on individual and dyadic levels (Cook, 1994). The SRM is the only structural equation model developed so far that integrates data on all relationships in the nuclear family and provides information on systematic sources of variance at each of the levels of analysis generally proposed as components of the family system (i.e. the family, the individual, and the relationship) (Cook, 1998). Data analysis using this model makes it possible to pinpoint which level (individual, dyadic, or family) contributes most to determining variability in the perceptions of support received by family members. For example, from a recently concluded study (Lanz, Tagliabue, & Rosnati, 2004) it emerged that the contribution of several effects, such as family effect and actor effect, is similar in the various relationships, while the partner effects and relationship effects vary in the different relationships. The stable actor effect in all the relationships indicates that the personal characteristics of the person expressing the judgement somehow determine the judgement itself, and this occurs in a similar manner both for parents and offspring. In contrast, the partner effect is very variable: particularly in relationships with mothers it is not very consistent while in relationships with fathers it is high, showing that the father's characteristics greatly impact the judgement that the others give of the support received from him. The relationship effect is very variable in all the relationships and, as already mentioned, is differentiated according to horizontal and vertical relationships. An interesting finding has to do with the family effect: this seems to impact to a high degree the judgements given by the family members. In other words, it seems that within the family its members have a shared way of judging the support received from others. The SRM and the application of structural equation models to family studies are not the definitive answer for analysis of the family but undoubtedly they are investigational instruments able to capture a part of the complexity of the family. When using such analytical techniques, it is fundamental to understand the importance of theory. The rationale for using these statistical techniques must come from the theoretical conceptualization of the constructs of interest. If the construct of interest is not defined as a system-level property these techniques may be irrelevant.

PROSPECTIVES FOR FUTURE RESEARCH

In the light of what has been discussed so far, in our opinion many questions arise as to how to succeed more fully in capturing the essence of the family as the intersection of genders and generations. First of all, we feel that the study of the transition to adulthood must be undertaken through longitudinal studies that capture not only the change in relationships but, above all, how family relationships manifest themselves over time.

Besides constantly pursuing an analysis by gender and generation with multiple informants—a path that has revealed itself to be very fruitful—it must also focus on the following items, with the appropriate methodologies:

- Influence of the quality of the marital relationship on the parent–child relationship and on late adolescents' and young adults' well-being. What are the connections between these relationships? And what are their consequences on offspring's transition to adulthood?[13]
- Fathers' new functions and roles: Recent theoretical thoughts and models on responsible and generative paternity propose which type of father? In a society of the affections, where the maternal function rules, how does the father reinvest and reconstruct himself by means of his own function?
- The sibling relationship: How do siblings, members of the family but also members of the same social generation, influence the quality of

family relations and make it possible to open different windows on the family context, and how much and how are they resources for the transition to adulthood?

• Openness to the social realm: In a society defined as being individualistic, where young people are stereotypically labelled as the mere carriers of individualistic and ephemeral values, why do some young people dedicate time and resources to involvement in the social context? How can the family promote or inhibit involvement in the social context? It is beyond doubt that investment in civic engagement and the citizenship of young people in the present opens or, in its absence, closes some possible future scenarios.

It is on these themes that, in our opinion, future research on family relations of adolescents and young adults will be played out. We are already involved in the pursuit of these themes. Although presented in the form of a list, in reality each of the topics proposed above is inextricably connected to the others: fully understanding the reality of families involved in their children's transition to adulthood implies a conjoint consideration of the relationships—intragenerational, intergenerational, and communitarian—that different family members are experiencing. As is well known by now, every researcher can allow him- or herself to understand only one or two pieces of the puzzle at a time without ever losing sight of the puzzle in its entirety and forcing him- or herself to put it together again in the most complete way possible.

Another crucial challenge for the researcher today is the realization of true multimethodological studies, but here the territory becomes impassable, the debate is lively: yet this is not the place to dedicate to this consideration more than this brief comment. A consideration of the specificity and complexity that characterize "the family organization" certainly invites experimentation with multiple and integrated research methodologies such as combine different levels of analysis and information of a diverse nature. It is necessary to design research projects in which qualitative and quantitative methods are not simply juxtaposed—creating, instead of a wealth of data, difficulty in recomposing the findings in a single picture—but rather to articulate and integrate the data among themselves so as to capture the different dimensions of family reality.

At the close of this work, our thoughts go to the hundreds of families of late adolescents and young adults whom we have met over the years: to them we extend our heartfelt gratitude for their availability, generosity, and suffering (at times) with which they opened to us their hearts and minds. Without their collaboration much of our work would not have been possible: we hope that our efforts will be able to help them and their children to experience a satisfactory transition to adulthood.

Notes

1 In the view of many disciplines, from social psychology to sociology, the theme of trust appears increasingly to be central to the analysis of the social bond itself. An awareness of the limits of utilitarian views of social exchange has motivated various authors to consider the trust one places in another person as being the crucial factor in forming and maintaining the social bond (Hollis, 1998). The literature on the subject of trust follows two different research currents: the first considers "trust" as such and refers to the fiduciary act of opening the "line" of credit that stands at the beginning of the relationship; the second considers trust in terms of trustworthiness and seems instead to refer more to the maintenance of the relationship (Rempel, Holmes, & Zanna, 1985). In the first case, trust seems to be located mostly on the affective plane, while in the second case it is found on the ethical plane.

2 It is worth noting that, in reality, the two orders of factors, affective and ethical, are not rigidly distinct but interpenetrate each other.

3 The authors explicitly define environment as cultural history, to be considered alongside family history and genetic influences. All three of these dimensions influence the horizontal axis that includes critical events of a social, familial, and individual nature. Family functioning is situated at the crossing of the horizontal and vertical axes. For example, when a critical event on the horizontal axis (such as the birth of a child) is linked to a problematical aspect in the intergenerational history (such as the presence of a handicapped child or a loss connected to a birth in past generations), the outcome of the transition is more uncertain. In an analogous fashion, the social and cultural history of a specific ethnic group may have a strong impact on family life. The effects felt down the generations of the tragic events involving the Jewish and Armenian peoples or, in more recent times, the disastrous ethnic conflicts in the ex-Yugoslavia and Africa come to mind, but also the apparently less dramatic and more common phenomenon of immigration.

4 A person is an adult when he or she is able to make a stable affective choice, work, contribute to making living conditions better in society, care for whatever he or she generates, and act responsibly towards the people with whom he or she interacts. In synthesis, we can say that an adult person is a generative person (Regalia & Marta, in press).

5 An example of fairness between generations is represented by the political redistribution of resources in accordance with a scale of needs translated into rights (civil, social, cultural) among which are to be found merit wants. For example, banks could adopt criteria for loans and financial investment with respect to young people (students and the employed) that no longer simply give preference to whoever can provide greater guarantees in the form of property or

personal income—that is, adults and the elderly – given that a "third party" could be found able to underwrite the risks involved.

6 For example, two couples obtain the same arithmetic mean in a satisfaction scale (score = 20) but in the first couple the husband scores 18 and the wife 22 while in the second couple the husband scores 10 and the wife 30. Using only the mean, the two couples could appear equally satisfied, but this is not true because in the second couple there is one person who is not satisfied at all (Lanz & Rosnati, 2002).

7 For example, it would be difficult to compare discrepancy scores obtained by a scale with a 7-point Likert scale and another scale with a 5-point Likert scale.

8 For example, a discrepancy of 10 points could occur between dyads anywhere along a scale with a 50-point range, both if the dyads score 40 and 50 or 3 and 13.

9 We remind the reader that in the first chapter we proposed the existence of two turning points in the long transition to adulthood: the first from early to late adolescence and the second from late adolescence to the phase of young adulthood.

10 The extreme differentiation of modern society has dissolved the synchronization between age and role transitions (Perlman & Giele, 1993), thus producing destandardization.

11 An "index of risk" was constructed with the same variables that the literature showed to be correlated with the adjustment of the adolescent. These variables are: self-esteem, socialization, and educational success. The index of risk was constructed with the MAUT (Multiattribute Utility Technology; Edwards & Newman, 1982). The group of adolescents was then divided into three subgroups (low, medium, and high risk) using the criterion of $\pm$ one σ (sigma) on the average of the index of risk scores.

12 The association between the two variables was calculated using the Spearman quadratic index of cograduation that measures the linear agreement between two ordinal variables.

13 On this subject we have an ongoing research project supported by a grant from the Italian Ministry of Education University and Research (2003118215_002 [2003]).

Appendix

Table 1. Databases: intact biological families

Study	Sample: #, Age	Research goal	Instruments	Analyses
A. YAF: Young Adult's Families (1988)	524 Family triads with a young-adult child (19–26 years)	• To study the level of perceived and ideal cohesion and adaptability in the family	• FACES III (Olson, 1986)	• ANOVA • MANOVA
B. FRAP: Family Relationships and Adolescents Project (1994)	595 Late adolescents (16–19 years) (269 girls, 326 boys) 419 Mothers (36–52 years) 403 Fathers (37–66 years) 279 family triads	• To study the family functioning and psychosocial risk for the adolescent • To analyse mothers' and fathers' influence on the adolescents' school and occupational expectations • To compare significant others of the generation of Italian adolescents and their parents, in order to verify the existence of similarities and differences in the choices of adolescents and their parents	• PACS (Barnes & Olson, 1985) • FSS (Olson & Wilson, 1982) • FES (Moos & Moos, 1976) • PASS (Scabini & Cigoli, 1992) • Self-esteem scale (Rosenberg, 1965) • Items on future expectations • Items on significant others and friends • Items on school • Sociodemographic items • A list of 12 significant others from which subjects were asked to indicate the 5 most significant people in order of importance	• t-test • ANOVAS • MANOVAS • Discrepancies scores • Regression • Path analysis • Log-linear

Study	Sample: #, Age	Research goal	Instruments	Analyses
C. YOFCA: Young and Family's Cohesion and Adaptability (1995)	762 Family triads with adolescents and young adults: • 195 families with a child aged from 16 to 18 • 307 families with a child aged from 19 to 21 • 270 families with a child aged from 21 to 24	• To monitor changes in level of perceived and ideal cohesion and adaptability in the family	• FACES III (Olson, 1985)	• ANOVA • MANOVA • Discrepancies scores
D. YAPI: Young Adult and the Process of Individuation (1996)	230 Family triads with a young-adult child (20–30 years)	• To study family relationships and their influence on children's future life planning	• PACS (Barnes & Olson, 1985) • FSS (Wilson & Olson, 1982) • FES (Moos & Moos, 1976) • PASS (Scabini & Cigoli, 1992)	• ANOVA • MANOVA • Discrepancies scores • Correlations
E. LAYAF: Late Adolescents' and Young-Adults' Families (1997)	75 Family triads with a late adolescent child (17–19 years) 110 Families with a young-adult child (20–26 years)	• To analyse continuity and discontinuity in the family relationships between the two phases of the life cycle	• PACS (Barnes & Olson, 1985) • FSS (Wilson & Olson, 1982) • FES (Moos & Moos, 1976) • PASS (Scabini & Cigoli, 1992)	• ANOVA • MANOVA • Discrepancies scores • Correlations

Study	Sample	Objectives	Instruments	Analyses

F. LAF: Late Adolescents' Families (1998)	1403 Late adolescents (17 to 22 years) (676 boys; 727 girls) 928 Mothers (30–71 years) 822 Fathers (35–72 years) 363 Siblings (20–40 years)	• To study family relationships and future orientation	• PACS (Barnes & Olson, 1985)
			• FSS (Wilson & Olson, 1982)
			• Decision-Making Scale (Steinberg, 1987)
			• Items regarding:
			  – conversational subjects
			  – areas of freedom
			  – future choices
			• Socio-demographic items
				• ANOVA
				• MANOVA
				• Discrepancies scores
				• Correlations

G. AFOFA: Adolescents' Future Orientation and Families (2000)	325 family triads with child (12–19 years)	• To analyse the influence of the family on adolescents' future planning • To study the process of autonomy	• List of hopes and fears for their own futures (version for adolescents) or their child's future (version for parents) • The subjects were further asked to assess: (1) the age when these hopes and fears could come true (this question measured temporal extension); (2) the extent to which the occurrence of each hope and fear depended on external or internal factors (this question measured control belief); and finally (3) the probability that each hope or fear could be actualized (this question measured level of realization). • PACS (Barnes & Olson, 1985)	• ANOVA • MANOVA • Discrepancies scores • Correlations • Thematic index • Regression

Study	Sample: #, Age	Research goal	Instruments	Analyses
H. YAVOFA: Young Adult Volunteers and their Families (2000)	155 family triads (father, mother and child) with a late adolescent/young adult (18–30 years) involved in volunteerism for at last 4 hours a week 155 triads with a late adolescent/young adult not involved in community-based action (17–30 years)	• To understand the family matrix and functioning of the late adolescents'/young adults' volunteers and non-volunteers	• Scale of altruism (Mehrabian & Epstein, 1972) • Prosociality Scale (Caprara et al., 1996) • Scale of values, *ad hoc* • PACS (Barnes & Olson, 1985) • PASS (Scabini & Cigoli, 1992) • Parental Style Scale, *ad hoc* • Scale of intergenerational transmission, *ad hoc* • Some short questions regarding exchange with the neighbourhood; engagement in voluntary organization; religious orientation	• ANOVA • MANOVA • Correlations • Regression • Cluster
I. CATA: Connectedness and Autonomy in the Transition to Adulthood (2000)	259 Italian families: parents, child (17–25 years) – late adolescent 17–19 years – young adult 20–25 years	• To verify how family relationships (support and style of decision) change from adolescence to young adulthood • To measure the agreement between parents and children as a marker of distance/ closeness between generations	• PASS (Scabini & Cigoli, 1992) • Style of Decision Making Scale (Steinberg, 1987)	• ANOVA • MANOVA • Correlations

| L. FAMCOLLEF: Family Collective Efficacy (2004) | 767 adolescents (14–22 years) (408 boys; 359 girls) 229 Mothers 304 Fathers | • To examine the impact that collective efficacy beliefs exert on important dimensions of family functioning
• To examine the extent to which parents' and children's collective efficacy is interrelated | • Collective Efficacy Scale (Caprara et al., 2004)
• Child Behavior Checklist (Achenbach, 1991)
• Depression Scale (Beck et al., 1961)
• PACS (Barnes & Olson, 1985)
• Monitoring Scale (Capaldi & Patterson, 1989)
• FSS (Wilson & Olson, 1982) | • ANOVA
• MANOVA
• Correlations |

FES, Family Environment Scale
FSS, Family Satisfaction Scale (Wilson & Olson, 1982)
PACS, Parent–Adolescent-Communication Scales (Barnes & Olson, 1985)
PASS, Parent–Adolescent Support Scales (Scabini & Cigoli, (1992).

Table 2. Databases: intact biological families, adopted families and separated families

Study	Sample: #, Age	Research goal	Instruments	Analyses
A. FRAP-BIOADO: Family Relationships and Adolescents Project—Biological and Adopted Families (1996)	103 adoptive and 150 non-adoptive triads (father, mother and child) with a late adolescent (16–19 years) (115 males and 138 females)	• To study the family functioning and psychosocial risk for the adolescent in biological and adopted families	• PACS (Barnes & Olson, 1985) • FSS (Wilson & Olson, 1982) • FES (Moos & Moos, 1976) • PASS (Scabini & Cigoli, 1992) • Self-esteem Scale (Rosenberg, 1965) • Items on significant others and friends • Items on school • Sociodemographic items	• t-test • ANOVAS • MANOVAS • Discrepancies scores • Regression
B. PACASE-TYPA: Parent–Child Communication and Adolescent Self-esteem in Different Types of Families (1999)	462 adolescents (11–18 years): – 160 from intact families – 145 from separated families – 157 from intercountry adoptive families and their parents	• To verify whether there are some differences in parent–child communication and in adolescents' self-esteem among adoptive, separated and intact non-adoptive families • To investigate the extent to which parent–child communication is related to adolescent self-esteem in 3 types of family	• PACS (Barnes & Olson, 1985) • Self-Esteem Scale (Rosenberg, 1965)	• ANOVAS • MANOVAS • Correlations

References

Abrams, D., & Hogg, M. (2004). Metatheory: Lessons from social identity research. *Personality and Social Psychology Review, 8*, 98–106.

Achenbach, T. M. (1991). *Manual for the Child Behaviour Checklist/4–18 and 1991 profile*. Burlington, VT: University of Vermont Department of Psychiatry.

Amato, P. R. (1994). Father–child relations, mother–child relations, and offspring psychological well-being in early adulthood. *Journal of Marriage and the Family, 56*(4), 1031–1042.

Amato, P. R., & Keith, B. (1991). Parental divorce and the well-being of children: A meta-analysis. *Psychological Bulletin, 110*(1), 26–46.

Amerio, P. (2004). *Problemi umani in comunità di massa [Human problems in the community]*. Turin: Einaudi.

Amerio, P. (Ed.) (1996). *Forme di solidarietà e linguaggi della politica [Forms of solidarity and political languages]*. Torino: Boringhieri.

Anderson, S., & Sabatelli, R. (1992). The Differentiation in the Family System Scale (DIFS). *American Journal of Family Therapy, 20*(1), 77–89.

Arnett, J. J. (2000). Emerging adulthood. *American Psychologist, 55*, 469–480.

Arnett, J. J. (2002). The psychology of globalization. *American Psychologist, 57*, 774–783.

Arnett, J. J. (2004). *Emerging adulthood: The winding road from late teens through the twenties*. Oxford: Oxford University Press.

Aro, M., & Palosaari, U. K. (1992). Parental divorce, adolescence, and transition to young adulthood. *American Journal of Orthopsychiatry, 62*, 421–429.

Bandura, A. (1997). *Self-efficacy: The exercise of control*. New York: Freeman/ Times Books/Henry Holt & Co.

Barber, B. K., & Buehler, C. (1996). Family cohesion and enmeshment: Different constructs, different effects. *Journal of Marriage and the Family, 58*(2), 433–441.

Barber, B. K., Olsen, J. A., & Shagle, S. (1994). Associations between parental psychological control and youth internalized and externalized behaviour. *Child Development, 65*, 1120–1136.

Barber, B. K., & Shagle, S. C. (1992). Adolescent problem behaviors: A social ecological analysis. *Family Perspective, 26*, 493–515.

Barnes, G., & Farrell, M. (1992). Parental support and control as predictors of adolescents' drinking, delinquency, and related problem behaviors. *Journal of Marriage and the Family, 54*(4), 763–776.

Barnes, H. L., & Olson, D. H. (1982). Parent–adolescent communication. In D. H. Olson, H. McCubbin, H. L. Barnes, A. Larsen, M. Muxen, & C. M. Wilson

(Eds.), *Family inventories. Family social science.* St. Paul, MN: University of Minnesota.

Barnes, H. L., & Olson, D. H. (1985). Parent–adolescent communication and the Circumplex Model. *Child Development, 56*(2), 438–447.

Bartle-Haring, S., Kenny, D. A., & Gavazzi, S. M. (1999). Multiple perspectives on family differentiation: Analyses by multitrait multimethod matrix and triadic social relations model. *Journal of Marriage and the Family, 61,* 491–503.

Beavers, W. R. (1982). Healthy, midrange, and severely dysfunctional families. In F. Walsh (Ed.), *Normal family processes* (pp. 45–66). New York: Guilford Press.

Beavers, W. R., & Hampson, R. B. (1993). Measuring family competence: The Beavers Systems Model. In F. Walsh (Ed.), *Normal family processes* (2nd edn) (pp. 73–103). New York: Guilford Press.

Beck, A. T., Ward, C. H., Mendelson, M., Mock, J., & Erbaugh, J. C. (1961). An inventory for measuring depression. *Archives of General Psychiatry, 4,* 561–571.

Beck, U. (1986). *Risk society: Towards a new modernity.* London: Sage Publications.

Bengston, V. L., & Achenbaum, W. A. (Eds.) (1993). *The changing contract across generations.* New York: Aldine De Gruyter.

Bengston, V. L., & Allen, K. (1993). The life course perspective applied to families over time. In P. G. Boss, W. J. Doherty, R. LaRossa, W. R. Schumm, & S. K. Steinmetz (Eds.), *Sourcebook of family theories and methods. A contextual approach* (pp. 469–504). New York: Plenum Press.

Bengston, V. L., & Cutler, N. E. (1976). Generations and intergenerational relations. In R. H. Binstock & E. Shanas (Eds.), *Handbook of aging and the social sciences* (pp. 130–159). San Diego, CA: Academic Press.

Benson, J. L. (1993). The measures of psychosocial development as predictors of depression among Greek Orthodox Christians in Oregon. *Dissertation Abstracts International, 53*(9-B), 4931.

Best, K., Hauser, S., & Allen, J. (1997). Predicting young-adult competencies: Adolescents and parents and individual influences. *Journal of Adolescence Research, 12,* 90–112.

Biggart, A., & Walther, A. (2001). Young adults' yo-yo transitions: Struggling for support between family and welfare state. Paper presented at the International Conference on 'Family forms and the young generation in Europe', Milan, September 2001.

Boccacin, L., & Marta, E. (Eds.) (2003). *Giovani-adulti, famiglia e volontariato. Percorsi di costruzione dell'identità. [Young adults, family and volunteerism. Paths of identity construction].* Milan: Unicopli.

Boszormenyi-Nagy, I., & Spark, G. (1973). *Invisible loyalties: Reciprocity in intergenerational family therapy.* Oxford: Harper & Row.

Branje, S. J. T., van Aken, M. A. G., & van Lieshout, C. F. M. (2002). Relational support in families with adolescents. *Journal of Family Psychology, 16*(3), 351–362.

Bray, J. H., Maxwell, S. E., & Cole, D. (1995). Multivariate statistics for family psychology research. *Journal of Family Psychology, 9*(2), 144–160.

Breunlin, D. C. (1988). Oscillation Theory and the family development. In C. J. Falicov (Ed.), *Family transition* (pp. 133–155). New York: Guilford Press.

Brewer, M. B. (1991). The social self: On being the same and different at the same time. *Personality and Social Psychology Bulletin, 17*(5), 475–482.

Bronfenbrenner, U. (1979). *The ecology of human development.* Cambridge, MA: Harvard University Press.

Buckley, W. (1976). *Sociology and modern systems theory.* Englewood Cliffs, NJ: Prentice-Hall.

Burleson, B. R. (2003). The experience and effects of emotional support: What the study of cultural and gender differences can tell us about close relationships, emotion, and interpersonal communication. *Personal Relationships, 10,* 1–23.

Burr, W. R. (1973). *Theory construction and the sociology of the family.* New York: John Wiley.

Campbell, D. T. (1958). Common fate, similarity and other indices of the status of aggregates of person as social entities. *Behavioral Science, 3,* 14–25.

Campbell, D. T., & Fiske, D. W. (1959). Convergent and discriminant validation by multitrait-multimethod matrix. *Psychological Bulletin, 56,* 81–105.

Campbell, K. (1970). *Mind and body.* New York: Macmillan.

Capaldi, D. M., & Patterson, G. R. (1989). *Psychometric properties of fourteen latent constructs from the Oregon Youth Study.* New York: Springer-Verlag.

Caprara, G. V., Pastorelli, C., & Bandura, A. (1996). La misura del disimpegno morale in età evolutiva. *Età Evolutiva, 51,* 18–29.

Caprara, G. V., Regalia, C., & Bandura, A. (2002). Longitudinal impact of perceived self-regulatory efficacy on violent conduct. *European Psychologist, 7,* 63–69.

Caprara, G. V., Regalia, C., Scabini, E., Barbaranelli, C., & Bandura, A. (2004). Assessment of filial, parental, marital, and collective family efficacy beliefs. *European Journal of Psychological Assessment, 20*(4), 247–261.

Caprara, G. V., Scabini, E., & Sgritta, G. B. (2003). The long transition to adulthood. An Italian view. In F. Pajares & T. Urdan (Eds.), *International perspectives on adolescence.* Greenwich: Information Age Publishing.

Carlson, C. (1989). Criteria for family assessment in research and intervention contexts. *Journal of Family Psychology, 3*(2), 158–176.

Carrà, E., & Marta, E. (1995). *Relazioni familiari e adolescenza [Family relationships and adolescence].* Milan: Franco Angeli.

Cashwell, C. S., & Vacc, N. A. (1996). Family functioning and risk behaviors: Influences on adolescent delinquency. *School Counselor, 44*(2), 105–114.

Cavalli, A., & Galland, O. (Eds.) (1993). *Senza fretta di crescere [The prolonged adolescence].* Naples: Liguori.

Chisholm, L., & Hurrelmann, K. (1994). Structured contradictions: Changes in status transition patterns and their implications for behavioral problems in adolescence. Unpublished manuscript.

Chun, Y. J., & MacDermid, S. M. (1997). Perceptions of family differentiation, individuation, and self-esteem among Korean adolescents. *Journal of Marriage and the Family, 59*(2), 451–462.

Cicognani, E., & Zani, B. (2003). *Genitori e adolescenti [Parents and adolescents].* Rome: Carocci.

Cigoli, V. (1995). Transizioni familiari [Family transitions]. In E. Scabini & P. Donati (Eds.), *Nuovo lessico familiare [New family lexicon]* (pp. 107–116). Milan: Vita e Pensiero.

Cigoli, V. (1997). *Intrecci familiari. Realtà interiore e scenario relazionale [Family plot. Interior reality and relational scene].* Milan: Raffaello Cortina Editore.

Cigoli, V., & Scabini, E. (forthcoming). *The family identity. Ties, symbols and transitions*. Mahwah, NJ: Lawrence Erlbaum Associates Inc.

Claes, M., Lacourse, E., Ercolani, A. P., Pierro, A., Leone, L., & Perucchini, P. (2001). Relazioni familiari, orientamento verso i coetanei e comportamenti devianti in adolescenza [Family relationships, orientation towards peers and deviant acts in adolescence.]. *Età Evolutiva, 70*, 30–44.

Cluff, R., Hicks, M., & Madsen, C. (1994). Beyond the Circumplex Model: A memorandum on curvilinearity. *Family Process, 33*(4), 455–470.

Cohen, E. A., Vasey, M. W., & Gavazzi, S. M. (2003). The dimensionality of family differentiation and the prediction of adolescent internalized distress. *Journal of Family Issues, 24*, 99–123.

Cohen, S., Underwood, L. G., & Gottlieb, B. H. (2000). *Social support measurement and intervention. A guide for health and social scientists*. New York: Oxford University Press.

Cole, D. A., & Jordan, A. E. (1989). Assessment of cohesion and adaptability in component family dyads: A question of convergent and discriminant validity. *Journal of Counseling Psychology, 36*(4), 456–463.

Cole, M. (1996). *Cultural psychology*. Cambridge, MA: Harvard University Press.

Coleman, P. K., & Karraker, K. H. (1998). Self-efficacy and parenting quality: Findings and future applications. *Developmental Review, 81*(1), 47–85.

Constantine, L. L. (1986). *Family paradigms*. New York: Guilford Press.

Cook, W. L. (1993). Interdependence and the interpersonal sense of control: An analysis of family relationships. *Journal of Personality and Social Psychology, 64*, 587–601.

Cook, W. L. (1994). A structural equation model of dyadic relationships within the family system. *Journal of Consulting and Clinical Psychology, 62*, 500–509.

Cook, W. L. (2000). Understanding attachment security in family context. *Journal of Personality and Social Psychology, 78*(2), 285–294.

Cook, W. L. (2001). Interpersonal influence in family systems: A social relations analysis. *Child Development, 72*, 1179–1197.

Cook, W. L., & Douglas, E. M. (1998). The looking-glass self in family context: A social relations analysis. *Journal of Family Psychology, 12*(3), 299–309.

Cooley, C. H. (1909). *Social organization*. Oxford: Scribners.

Cooper, C. R., Grotevant, H. D., & Condon, S. (1983). Individuality and connectedness in the family as a context for adolescent identity formation and role-taking skill. *New Directions for Child Development, 22*, 43–59.

Cordon, J. A. (1997). Youth residential independence and autonomy: A comparative study. *Journal of Family Issues, 18*, 576–607.

Costanzo, P. R., & Woody, E. Z. (1985). Domain-specific parenting styles and their impact on the child's development of particular deviance: The example of obesity proneness. *Journal of Social and Clinical Psychology, 3*, 425–445.

Cox, M., Brooks-Gunn, J., & Paley, B. (1999). Perspectives on conflict and cohesion in families. In M. Cox & J. Brooks-Gunn (Eds.), *Conflict and cohesion in families. Causes and consequences* (pp. 87–104). Mahwah, NJ: Lawrence Erlbaum Associates Inc.

Crespi, I. (2004). Socialization and gender roles within the family: A study on adolescents and their parents in Great Britain. *The Annals of the Marie Curie Fellowship* (Vol. 3, pp. 124–131). Brussels: European Commission.

Csikszentmihalyi, M., Rathunde, K., & Whalen, S. (1993). *Talented teenagers: The roots of success and failure*. New York: Cambridge University Press.

Cumsille, P., & Epstein, N. (1994). Family cohesion, family adaptability, social support, and adolescent depressive symptoms in outpatient clinic families. *Journal of Family Psychology*, *8*(2), 202–214.

Deal, J. E. (1995). Utilizing data from multiple family members: A within-family approach. *Journal of Marriage and the Family*, *57*(4), 1109–1121.

Deal, J. E., Halverson, C. F., & Wampler, K. S. (1989). Parental agreement on child-rearing orientations: Relations to parental, marital, family, and child characteristics. *Child Development*, *60*, 1025–1034.

Dekovic, M., & Janssens, J. M. (1992). Parents' child-rearing style and child's sociometric status. *Developmental Psychology*, *28*(5), 925–932.

Delsing, M. J. M. H., Oud, J. H. L., De Bruyn, E. E. J., & van Aken, M. A. G. (2003). Current and recollected perceptions of family relationships: The Social Relations Model approach applied to members of three generations. *Journal of Family Psychology*, *17*(4), 445–459.

Doherty, W. J., Boss, P. G., LaRossa, R., Schumm, W. R., & Steinmetz, S. K. (1993). *Sourcebook of family theories and methods: A contextual approach*. New York: Plenum Press.

Doherty, W. J., Kouneski, E. F., & Erickson, M. F. (1998). Responsible fathering: An overview and conceptual framework. *Journal of Marriage and the Family*, *60*(2), 277–292.

Dollahite, D. C., & Hawkins, A. J. (1998). Conceptual ethic of generative father. *Journal of Men's Studies*, *7*, 109–132.

Dollahite, D. C., Slife, B. D., & Hawkins, A. J. (1998). Family generativity and generative counseling: Helping families to keep faith with the next generation. In D. P. McAdams & E. de St Aubin (Eds.), *Generativity and adult development: How and why we care for the next generation* (pp. 449–481). Washington, DC: American Psychological Association.

Donati, P. (1991). *Secondo rapporto sulla famiglia in Italia. [Second report on the family in Italy]*. Cinisello Balsamo: Edizioni Paoline.

Duck, S. (1988). *Relating to others*. Homewood, IL: Dorsey Press.

Duck, S. (1997). *Handbook of personal relationships: Theory, research and interventions*. New York: John Wiley & Sons, Inc.

Duvall, E. M. (1977). *Family development*. Philadelphia: Lippincott.

Edwards, W., & Newman, R. (1982). *Multiattribute evaluation* (Vol. 26). Sage University Paper Series on Quantitative Application in the Social Sciences, Beverly Hills, CA: Sage Publications.

Eisenberg, N. (1991). Meta-analytic contributions to the literature on prosocial behavior. *Personality and Social Psychology Bulletin*, *17*, 273–282.

Eisenberg, N., & Fabes, R. A. (1998). Prosocial development. In W. Damon & N. Eisenberg (Eds.), *Handbook of child psychology, Vol. 3: Social, emotional and personality development* (5th edn, pp. 701–778). New York: Wiley and Sons.

Eisenberg, N., & Miller, P. A. (1987). The relation of empathy to prosocial and related behaviors development. *Psychological Bulletin*, *1*, 91–119.

Epstein, N. B., Bishop, D. S., & Baldwin, L. M. (1982). McMaster Model of Family Functioning: A view of the normal family. In F. Walsh (Ed.), *Normal family processes* (pp. 115–141). New York: Guilford Press.

Erikson, E. (1982). *The life cycle completed*. New York: Norton.

Falicov, C. J. (1988). *Family sociology and family therapy contributions to the family development framework: A comparative analysis and thoughts on future trends.* New York: Guildford Press.

Farina, M., & Galimberti, C. (1993). Relazioni intergenerazionali e ipotesi di autonomizzazione nella famiglia del giovane adulto [Intergenerational relationships and hypotheses for the young-adult autonomization in the family]. *Età Evolutiva, 45,* 35–46.

Farrell, M., & Barnes, G. (1993). Family system and social support: A test of the effects of cohesion and adaptability on the functioning of parents and adolescents. *Journal of Marriage and the Family, 55*(1), 119–132.

Feetham, S. L. (1988). Developing programs of research of families. Unpublished manuscript.

Fisher, L., Kokes, R. F., Ransom, D. C., Philips, S. L., & Rudd, P. (1985). Alternative strategies for creating "relational" family data. *Family Process, 24,* 213–224.

Flanagan, C., Jonsson, B., Botcheva, L., Csapo, B., Bowes, J., Macek, P., Averina, I., & Sheblanova, E. (1999). Adolescents and the "social contract": Developmental roots of citizenship in seven countries. In M. Yates & J. Youniss (Eds.), *Roots of civic identity: International perspectives on community service and activism in youth* (pp. 135–155). New York: Cambridge University Press.

Fletcher, C., Elder, G. H. J., & Mekos, D. (2000). Parental influences on adolescent involvement in community activities. *Journal of Research on Adolescence, 10*(1), 29–48.

Foster, J., & Fernandes, M. (1996). *Young people and volunteering: A literature review.* London: The Volunteer Process Model Centre.

Fournier, D., Olson, D. H., & Druckman, J. (1983). Assessing marital and premarital relationships. The Prepare-Enrich Inventorie. In E. Felsinger (Ed.), *Marriage and family assessment* (pp. 229–250). Beverly Hills, CA: Sage Publications.

Fuhrman, T., & Holmbeck, G. (1995). A contextual-moderator analysis of emotional autonomy and adjustment in adolescence. *Child Development, 66*(3), 793–811.

Furlong, A., & Cartmel, F. (1997). *Young people and social change.* Buckingham: Open University Press.

Gavazzi, S. M. (1993). The relation between family differentiation levels in families with adolescents and the severity of presenting problems. *Family Relations, 42*(4), 463–468.

Gillis, A. J. (1993). The relationship of definition of health, perceived health status, self-efficacy, parental health-promoting lifestyle, and selected demographics to health-promoting lifestyle in adolescent females. *Dissertation Abstracts International, 54*(5–B), 2439.

Glass, J., & Polisar, D. (1987). A method and metric for assessing similarity among dyads. *Journal of Marriage and the Family, 49*(3), 663–668.

Godbout, J. (1992). *L'Esprit du don [The gift spirit].* Montreal: Editions du Boreal.

Goldin, P. C. (1969). A review of children's reports of parent behaviors. *Psychological Bulletin, 71,* 222–236.

Goldscheider, F. (1997). Recent changes in U.S. young adult living arrangements in comparative perspective. *Journal of Family Issues, 18,* 708–724.

Graber, J. A., & Brooks-Gunn, J. (1999). Sometimes I think that you don't like me:

How mothers and daughters negotiate the transition into adolescence. In M. Cox & J. Brooks-Gunn (Eds.), *Conflict and cohesion in families: Causes and consequences* (pp. 207–242). Mahwah, NJ: Lawrence Erlbaum Associates Inc.

Graber, J. A., & Dubas, J. S. (1996). *Leaving home: Understanding the transition to adulthood.* San Francisco: Jossey-Bass.

Green, R. J., & Werner, P. (1996). Intrusiveness and closeness-caregiving: Rethinking the concept of family enmeshment. *Family Process, 35*(2), 115–136.

Greene, A. L., & Grimsley, M. D. (1990). Age and gender differences in adolescents' preferences for parental advice: Mum's the word. *Journal of Adolescent Research, 5*(4), 396–413.

Grotevant, H. D. (1989). The role of theory in guiding family assessment. *Journal of Family Psychology, 3*(2), 104–117.

Grotevant, H. D., & Cooper, C. R. (1986). Individuation in the family relationships: A perspective of individual differences in the development of identity and role-taking skill in adolescence. *Human Development, 29*, 82–100.

Grube, J. A., & Piliavin, J. A. (2000). Role identity, organizational experiences, and volunteer performance. *Personality and Social Psychology Bulletin, 26*, 1108–1119.

Guglielmetti, C. (2003). I giovani volontari e le loro famiglie [Young adult volunteers and their families]. In E. Marta & E. Scabini (Eds.), *Giovani volontari [Young adult volunteers]* (pp. 100–128). Florence: Giunti.

Haley, J. (1973). *Uncommon therapy: The psychiatric techniques of Milton H. Erickson, MD.* New York: Norton.

Hartos, J. L., & Power, T. G. (2000). Association between mother and adolescent reports for assessing relations between parent–adolescent communication and adolescent adjustment. *Journal of Youth and Adolescence, 29*(4), 441–450.

Hauser, S. T., Vieyra, M. A., Jacobson, A. M., & Wertlieb, D. (1985). Vulnerability and resilience in adolescence: Views from the family. *Journal of Early Adolescence, 5*(1), 81–100.

Havighurst, R. J. (1972). *Developmental tasks and education* (3rd edn). New York: David McKay.

Hawkins, A., & Dollahite, D. (1997). *Generative fathering: Beyond deficit perspective.* Thousand Oaks, CA: Sage.

Hawley, A. (1986). *Human ecology: A theoretical essay.* Chicago: University of Chicago Press.

Heelas, P., Lash, S., & Morris, P. (Eds.) (1996). *Critical reflections on authority and identity at a time of uncertainty.* London: Blackwell Publishers.

Hein, C., & Lewko, J. H. (1994). Gender differences in factors related to parenting style: A study of high performing science students. *Journal of Adolescence Research, 9*, 262–281.

Heinz, W. R. (1996). L'ingresso nella vita attiva in Germania e Gran Bretagna [Entering active life in Germany and Great Britain]. In A. Cavalli & O. Galland (Eds.), *Senza fretta di crescere [The prolonged adolescence]* (pp. 83–102). Arles: Hubert Nissen Editeur.

Hess, L. (1994). Changing family patterns in Western Europe: Opportunity and risk factors for adolescent development. Unpublished manuscript.

Hetherington, E. M. (1991). The role of individual differences and family relationships in children's coping with divorce and remarriage. In P. A. Cowan &

E. M. Hetherington (Eds.), *Family transitions*. Hillsdale, NJ: Lawrence Erlbaum Associates Inc.

Hill, R. (1949a). *Families under stress*. New York: Harper & Brothers.

Hill, R. (1949b). *Family under stress*. New York: Harper-Row.

Hinde, R. A. (1988). Continuities and discontinuities: Conceptual issues and methodological considerations. In M. Rutter (Ed.), *Studies of psychosocial risk: The power of longitudinal data* (pp. 367–383). New York: Cambridge University Press.

Hinde, R. A. (1997). *Relationships: A dialectical perspective*. London: Psychology Press.

Hinde, R. A., Finkenauer, C., & Auhagen, A. E. (2001). Relationships and the self-concept. *Personal Relationships, 8*(2), 187–204.

Hoge, R. D., Andrews, D. A., & Leschied, A. W. (1996). An investigation of risk and protective factors in a sample of youthful offenders. *Journal of Child Psychology and Psychiatry and Applied Disciplines, 37*(4), 419–424.

Holahan, C. J., Valentiner, D. P., & Moos, R. H. (1994). Parental support and psychological adjustment during the transition to young adulthood in a college sample. *Journal of Family Psychology, 8*(2), 215–223.

Hollis, M. (1998). *Trust within reason*. Cambridge: Cambridge University Press.

Hosley, C. A., & Montemayor, R. (1997). Fathers and adolescents. In E. Lamb (Ed.), *The role of the father in child development* (3rd edn, pp. 162–178). New York: John Wiley & Sons, Inc.

Hurrelmann, K. (1989). The social world of adolescence: A sociological perspective. In K. Hurrelmann & E. Uwe (Eds.), *The social world of adolescence* (pp. 3–26). Oxford: Walter de Gruyter.

Hurrelmann, K., & Chisholm, L. (1993). Structured contradictions: Changes in status transition patterns and their implications for behavioral problems in adolescence. Unpublished manuscript.

Hurrelmann, K., & Engel, U. (1989). *The social world of adolescence*. Berlin: De Gruyter.

Iacovou, M., & Berthoud, R. (2001). *Young people's lives: A map of Europe*. Colchester, UK: University of Essex, Institute for Social and Economic Research.

Jackson, S., Bijstra, J., Oostra, L., & Bosma, H. (1998). Adolescents' perceptions of communication with parents relative to specific aspects of relationships with parents and personal development. *Journal of Adolescence, 21*(3), 305–322.

Janoski, T., & Wilson, J. (1995). Pathways to voluntarism: Family socialization and status transmission models. *Social Forces, 74*(1), 271–292.

Kenny, D. A. (2000). Dyadic indices. Unpublished manuscript.

Kenny, D. A., & Acitelli, L. K. (1994). Measuring similarity in couples. *Journal of Family Psychology, 8*(4), 417–431.

Kenny, D. A., & Judd, C. M. (1986). Consequences of violating the independence assumption in analysis of variance. *Psychological Bulletin, 99*(3), 422–431.

Kenny, D. A., & Kashy, D. A. (1992). Analysis of the multitrait-multimethod matrix by confirmatory factor analysis. *Psychological Bulletin, 112*(1), 165–172.

Kenny, D. A., & La Voie, L. (1984). The Social Relations Model. In L. Berkowitz (Ed.), *Advances in experimental social psychology* (Vol. 18, pp. 14–182). San Diego, CA: Academic Press.

Kerckhoff, A. C., & Macrae, J. (1992). Leaving the parental home in Great Britain. *Sociological Quarterly, 33*(2), 281–301.

Kerns, K. A., Aspelmeier, J. E., Gentzler, A. L., & Grabill, C. M. (2001). Parent–child attachment and monitoring in middle childhood. *Journal of Family Psychology*, *15*(1), 69–81.

King, M., Walder, L., & Pavey, S. (1970). Personality change as a function of volunteer experience in a psychiatric hospital. *Journal of Consulting and Clinical Psychology*, *35*(3), 423–425.

Kirkcaldy, B., Siefen, G., & Furnham, A. (2003). Gender, anxiety-depressivity and self-image among adolescents. *European Psychiatry*, *18*, 50–58.

Kirkpatrick-Johnson, M., Beebe, T., Mortimer, J. T., & Snyder, M. (1998). Volunteerism in adolescence: A process perspective. *Journal of Research on Adolescence*, *8*, 309–332.

Klein, D. M., & White, J. M. (1996). *Family theories: An introduction*. Thousand Oaks, CA: Sage.

Kotre, J. (1984). *Outliving the self: Generativity and the interpretation of lives*. Baltimore, MD: Johns Hopkins University Press.

Kotre, J., & Kotre, K. B. (1998). Intergenerational buffers: "The damage stops here". In D. P. McAdams & E. De St Aubin (Eds.), *Generativity and adult development: How and why we care for the next generation* (pp. 367–389). Washington, DC: American Psychological Association.

Kurdek, L. A., Fine, M. A., & Sinclair, R. J. (1995). School adjustment in sixth graders: Parenting transition, family climate, and peer norm effects. *Child Development*, *66*, 430–445.

Lacan, J. (1977). *Ecrits: A selection*. London: Norwood.

Lanz, M. (1997). Parent–offspring Communication Scale: Applicazione ad un campione italiano [Parent–offspring Communication Scale: a validation on an Italian sample]. *Bolletino di Psicologia Applicata*, *224*, 33–38.

Lanz, M. (1998). Dall'adolescenza alla giovinezza: Continuità e cambiamenti [From adolescence to youth: Continuity and changes]. *Età Evolutiva*, *61*, 56–63.

Lanz, M. (2000). From adolescence to young adulthood: A family transition. In C. Violato, E. Oddonne-Paolucci, & M. Genius (Eds.), *The changing family and child development* (pp. 132–146). Aldershot, UK: Ashgate.

Lanz, M., Iafrate, R., Rosnati, R., & Scabini, E. (1999). Parent–child communication and adolescents' self-esteem in separated, inter-country adoptive and intact-nonadoptive families. *Journal of Adolescence*, *22*, 785–794.

Lanz, M., & Rosnati, R. (2002). *Metodologia della ricerca sulla famiglia [The methodology of family research]*. Milan: LED.

Lanz, M., Rosnati, R., Iafrate, R., & Marta, E. (1999). Significant others in Italian families with late adolescents. *Psychological Reports*, *84*, 459–466.

Lanz, M., Rosnati, R., Marta, E., & Scabini, E. (2001). Adolescents' future: A comparison of adolescents' and their parents' views. In J. E. Nurmi (Ed.), *Navigating through adolescence: European perspective* (pp. 169–198). New York: Routledge.

Lanz, M., Tagliabue, S., & Rosnati, R. (2004). Il Social Relations Model nello studio delle relazioni familiari [The Social Relations Model in the family relationships studies]. *Testing Psicometria Metodologia*, *11*(4), 197–214.

Larsen, A., & Olson, D. H. (1990). Capturing the complexity of family systems: Integrating family theory, family scores, and family analysis. In T. W. Draper & A. C. Marcos (Eds.), *Family variables: Conceptualization, measurement, and use. New perspectives on family* (pp. 19–47). Thousand Oaks, CA: Sage Publications.

Laslett, P., & Wall, R. (1972). *Household and family in past time*. Cambridge: Cambridge University Press.

Lavee, Y. (1988). Linear Structural Relationships (LISREL) in family research. *Journal of Marriage and the Family, 50*, 937–948.

Levine, J., & Moreland, R. (1998). Small groups. In D. Gilbert & S. Fiske (Eds.), *The Handbook of Social Psychology* (Vol. 2, pp. 415–469). New York: McGraw-Hill.

Lewin, K. (1946). Action research and minority problems. *Journal of Social Issues, 2*, 34–46.

Lewin, K. (1948). *Resolving social conflicts: Selected papers on group dynamics*. Oxford: Harper.

Lewin, K. (1951). *Field theory in social science: Selected theoretical papers*. Oxford: Harper.

Lewis, C., & Lamb, M. E. (2003). Fathers' influences on children's development: The evidence from two-parent families. *European Journal of Psychology of Education, 18*(2), 211–228.

Litovsky, V. G., & Duserk, J. B. (1985). Perception of child rearing and self-concept development during the early adolescent years. *Journal of Youth and Adolescence, 14*, 373–387.

McAdams, D. P., & de St Aubin, E. (1992). A theory of generativity and its assessment through self-report, behavioral acts, and narrative themes in autobiography. *Journal of Personality and Social Psychology, 62*, 1003–1015.

McAdams, D. P., & de St Aubin, E. (1998). *Generativity and adult development: How and why we care for the next generation*. Washington, DC: American Psychological Association.

McAdoo, H. P. (1993). Ethnic families: strengths that are found in diversity. In H. P. McAdoo (Ed.), *Family ethnicity: Strength in diversity* (pp. 3–14). Thousand Oaks, CA: Sage Publications.

Maccoby, E. E., & Martin, J. A. (1983). Socialization in the context of the family: Parent–child interaction. In P. H. Mussen (Ed.), *Handbook of Child Psychology* (pp. 1–101). New York: Wiley.

McCubbin, H. I., & Patterson, J. M. (1981). Family stress and adaptation to crises: A double ABCDX Model of family behavior. Paper presented at the Annual Meeting of the National Council on Family Relations, Milwaukee, WI, 13–17 October 1981.

McGoldrick, M., Heiman, H., & Carter, B. (1993a). I mutamenti nel ciclo di vita della famiglia [Family life cycle and family dynamics]. In F. Walsh (Ed.), *Ciclo vitale e dinamiche familiari [The changes in the family cycle]*. Milan: Franco Angeli.

McGoldrick, M., Heiman, M., & Carter, B. (1993b). The changing family life cycle: A perspective on normality. In F. Walsh (Ed.), *Normal family processes* (pp. 405–443). New York: Guilford Press.

Mackie, A. J. (1985). Families with adopted adolescents. *Journal of Adolescence, 35*, 167–178.

Manganelli Rattazzi, A. M., & Capozza, D. (1993). Famiglia, ruoli sessuali e aspettative giovanili [Family, sexual roles and youth expectations]. In M. Cusinato (Ed.), *Ruoli e vissuti familiari. Nuovi approcci* (pp. 23–49). Florence: Giunti.

Mantovani, G. (2000). *Exploring borders: Understanding culture and psychology.* New York: Routledge.

Marks, S. (1977). Multiple roles and role strain: Some notes on human energy, time and commitment. *American Social Review, 42,* 921–936.

Marsiglio, W., Amato, P., Day, R. D., & Lamb, M. E. (2000). Scholarship on fatherhood in the 1990s and beyond. *Journal of Marriage and the Family, 62,* 1173–1191.

Marta, E. (1997). Parent–adolescent interaction and psycho-social risk in adolescence: An analysis of communication, support, and gender. *Journal of Adolescence, 20,* 473–487.

Marta, E., & Pozzi, M. (in press). Young volunteers, family and social capital: From the care of family bonds to the care of community bonds. In M. Hofer, A. Sliwka, & M. Dietrich (Eds.), *Perspectives on citizenship education: Theory – Research – Practice.* Munster/New York: Waxmann.

Marta, E., & Scabini, E. (2003). *Giovani volontari. Impegnarsi, crescere e far crescere. [Young volunteers. Getting involved, growing and helping others to grow].* Florence: Giunti.

Martin, J., & Cole, D. (1993). Adaptability and cohesion of dyadic relationships in families with developmentally disabled children. *Journal of Family Psychology, 7*(2), 186–196.

Mehrabian, A., & Epstein, N. (1972). A measure of emotional empathy. *Journal of Personality, 40,* 525–543.

Meltzer, D., & Harris, M. (1983). *Child, family and community: A psychoanalytical model of learning process.* Paris: OECD.

Miller, B. C., & Heaton, T. B. (1991). Age at first sexual intercourse and the timing of marriage and childbirth. *Journal of Marriage and the Family, 53*(3), 719–732.

Miller, J. B., & Lane, M. (1991). Relations between young adults and their parents. *Journal of Adolescence, 14*(2), 179–194.

Moore, C. W., & Allen, J. P. (1996). The effects of volunteering on the young volunteer. *Journal of Primary Prevention, 17*(2), 231–258.

Moos, R. H., & Moos, B. S. (1976). A typology of family social environment. *Family Process, 15,* 357–371.

Moos, R. H., & Moos, B. S. (1981). *Family Environment Scale manual.* Palo Alto, CA: Consulting Psychologist Press.

Mortimer, J. T., & Larson, R. W. (2002). *The changing adolescence experience: Societal trends and the transition to adulthood.* Cambridge: Cambridge University Press.

Moscovici, S. (1994). *Psychologie sociale des relations à autrui [Social Psychology of relationships with others].* Paris: Nathan.

Murdock, G. P. (1949). *Social structure.* Oxford: Macmillan.

Muris, P., Meesters, C., & van den Berg, S. (2003). Internalizing and externalizing problems as correlates of self-reported attachment style and perceived parental rearing in normal adolescents. *Journal of Child and Family Studies, 12*(2), 171–183.

Newman, B., & Newman, P. (1995). *Development through life: A psychological approach* (6th edn). Pacific Grove, CA: Brooks/Cole.

Noack, P., Kerr, M., & Olah, A. (1999). Family relations in adolescence. *Journal of Adolescence, 22*(6), 713–717.

Noller, P., & Callan, V. J. (1990). Adolescents' perceptions of the nature of their communication with parents. *Journal of Youth and Adolescence, 19*, 349–362.

Noller, P., & Callan, V. J. (1991). *The adolescent in the family*. Florence, KY: Taylor & Frances/Routledge.

Nurmi, J. E. (1989a). Adolescents' orientation to the future: Development of interest and plans, and related attributions and affects, in the life-span context. Paper presented at the Commentationes Scientiarum Socialium, Helsinki.

Nurmi, J. E. (1989b). Development of orientation to the future during early adolescence: A four year longitudinal study and two cross-sectional comparisons. *International Journal of Psychology, 24*(2), 195–214.

Nurmi, J.-E. (1987). Age, sex, class, and quality of family interaction as determinants of adolescents' future interaction: A developmental task interpretation. *Adolescence, 22*(88), 977–991.

Nurmi, J.-E. (1991). How do adolescents see their future? A review of the development of future orientation and planning. *Developmental Review, 11*(1), 1–59.

Offer, D., Ostrov, E., & Howard, K. I. (1981). The mental health professional's concept of the normal adolescent. *Archives of General Psychiatry, 38*(2), 149–152.

Oliveri, M. E., & Reiss, D. (1982). Family styles of construing the social environment: A perspective on variation among nonclinical families. In F. Walsh (Ed.), *Normal family processes* (pp. 94–114). New York: Guilford Press.

Olson, D. H. (1969). Development and evaluation of family interaction procedure. Paper presented at the American Psychological Association, Washington, June 1969.

Olson, D. H. (1976). *Treating relationships*. Lake Mills, IO: Graphic Publishing Co.

Olson, D. H. (1986). Circumplex model VII: Validation studies and FACES III. *Family Process, 25*, 337–351.

Olson, D. H. (1993). Circumplex model of marital and family systems: Assessing family functioning. In W. F. Walsh (Ed.), *Normal family processes* (2nd edn, pp. 104–137). New York: Guilford Press.

Olson, D. H., Sprenkle, D., & Russell, C. (1979). Circumplex model of marital and family systems: Cohesion and adaptability dimensions, family types, and clinical applications. *Family Process, 18*(1), 3–28.

Olson, D. H., & Wilson, M. (1982). Family Satisfaction Scale. Family inventories. In D. Olson, H. Mc Cubbin, H. L. Barnes, A. Larsen, M. Muxen, & C. M. Wilson (Eds.), *Family inventories. Family social science*. St. Paul, MN: University of Minnesota.

Omoto, A. M., & Snyder, M. (1990). Basic research in action: Volunteerism and society's response to AIDS. *Personality and Social Psychology Bulletin, 16*(1), 152–165.

Palmonari, A. (Ed.) (1997). *Psicologia dell'adolescenza [Psychology of adolescence]*. Bologna: Il Mulino.

Pancer, S. M., Pratt, M., & Hunsberger, B. (1998). Community and political involvement in adolescence: What distinguishes the activists from the uninvolved? Paper presented at the 7th Biennal Meeting of the Society for Research in Adolescence, San Diego, CA, February 1998.

Pancer, S. M., & Pratt, M. W. (1999). Social and family determinants of community service involvement in Canadian youth. In M. Yates & J. Youniss (Eds.), *Roots of civic identity: International perspectives on community service and activism in youth* (pp. 32–55). New York: Cambridge University Press.

Perlman, R., & Giele, J. Z. (1983). An unstable triad: Dependents' demands, family resources, community supports. In R. Perlman (Ed.), *Family home care: Critical issues for services and policies* (pp. 12–44). New York: The Haworth Press.

Pietropolli Charmet, G. (2000). *I nuovi adolescenti [New adolescents]*. Milan: Cortina.

Polanyi, M. (1974). Scientific thought and social reality. *Psychological Issues, 8*(4, Mono 32), 157.

Raskoff, S., & Sundeen, R. (1994). The ties that bond: Teenage volunteers in the United States. Paper presented at the International Sociological Association Meeting, Bielefeld, Germany.

Regalia, C., & Marta, E. (in press). *Identità in azione [Identity in action]*. Rome: Carocci.

Regalia, C., Pastorelli, C., Barbaranelli, C., & Gerbino, M. (2001). Convinzioni di efficacia personale filiale [Beliefs of filial self-efficacy]. *Giornale Italiano di Psicologia, 3*, 575–593.

Reiss, D. (1981). *The family construction of reality*. Cambridge, MA: Harvard University Press.

Rempel, J. K., Holmes, J. G., & Zanna, M. P. (1985). Trust in close relationships. *Journal of Personality and Social Psychology, 49*, 95–112.

Ricolfi, L. (1984). Il paradigma della reversibilità [Reversibility paradigm]. In A. Tarrozzi & G. Bongiovanni (Eds.), *Le imperfette utopie [Faulty utopia]*. Milan: Franco Angeli.

Risch, S. C., Jodl, K. M., & Eccles, J. S. (2004). Role of the father–adolescent relationship in shaping adolescents' attitudes toward divorce. *Journal of Marriage and Family, 66*, 46–58.

Robinson, J. L., Zahan-Waxler, C., & Emde, R. (1994). Patterns of development in early empathic behavior: Environmental and child constitutional influences. *Social Development, 3*, 125–145.

Rosen, B. C., & Aneshensel, C. S. (1978). Sex differences in the educational-occupational expectation process. *Social Force, 57*(1), 64–186.

Rosenberg, M. (1965). *Society and the adolescent self-image*. Princeton, NJ: Princeton University Press.

Rosnati, R. (1995). Adolescenti e aspettative per il futuro: Una prospettiva familiare [Adolescents and future expectations: A family perspective]. In E. Carrà & E. Marta (Eds.), *Relazioni familiari e adolescenza [Family relationships and adolescence]* (pp. 78–98). Milan: Franco Angeli.

Rosnati, R. (1996). Comunicazione e supporto familiari e aspettative per il futuro in età adolescenziale [Family support and communication, and future expectations in adolescence]. *Archivio di Psicologia, Neurologia e Psichiatria, 2–3*, 280–299.

Rosnati, R., & Marta, E. (1997). Parent–child relationships as protective factors in preventing adolescents' psycho-social risk in adoptive and non-adoptive families. *Journal of Adolescence, 20*, 617–631.

Rossi, A., & Rossi, P. (1990). *Of human bonding: Parent–child relations across the life course*. New York: Aldine De Gruyter.

Rossi, G. (1997). The nestlings: Why young adult stay at home longer. The Italian case. *Journal of Family Issues, 18*, 627–644.

Rowntree, B. S. (1903). *Poverty: A study of town life*. London: Macmillan.

Ruble, D., & Seidman, E. (1996). Social transitions: Windows into social psychological processes. In T. Higging & A. Kruglanski (Eds.), *Social psychology: Handbook of basic principles* (pp. 830–856). New York: Guilford Press.

Sabatelli, R. M., & Bartle, S. E. (1995). Survey approaches to the assessment of family functioning: Conceptual, operational, and analytical issues. *Journal of Marriage and the Family*, *57*(4), 1025–1039.

Sabatelli, R., & Mazor, A. (1985). Differentiation, individuation, and identity formation: The integration of family and individual developmental perspectives. *Adolescence*, *20*(79), 619–633.

Sahlins, M. (1972). *Stone age economics*. London: Tavistock.

Sandberg, D. E., Ehrhardt, A. A., Ince, S. E., & Meyer-Bahlburg, H. F. (1991). Gender differences in children's and adolescents' career aspirations: A follow-up study. *Journal of Adolescent Research*, *6*(3), 371–386.

Saraceno, C. (1988). *Sociologia della famiglia [Sociology of the family]*. Bologna: Il Mulino.

Scabini, E. (1995). *Psicologia sociale della famiglia [Family social psychology]*. Turin: Bollati Boringhieri.

Scabini, E. (2000a). New aspects of family relations. In C. Violato & E. Oddone-Paolucci (Eds.), *The changing family and child development* (pp. 3–24). Aldershot, UK: Ashgate Publishing.

Scabini, E. (2000b). Parent–child relationship in Italian families: Connectedness and autonomy in the transition to adulthood. *Psicologia: Teoria e Pesquisa*, *16*(1), 23–30.

Scabini, E. (2001). Adolescenti e relazioni familiari [Adolescents and family relationships]. In A. Cavalli & C. Facchini (Eds.), *Scelte cruciali. Indagine IARD su giovani e famiglie di fronte alle scelte alla fine della scuola secondaria [Crucial choices. IARD report on young and families facing choices at the end of the secondary school]* (pp. 171–227). Bologna: Il Mulino.

Scabini, E., & Cigoli, V. (1992). La scala di supporto genitori–figli [Parent–child Support Scale]. Unpublished manuscript.

Scabini, E., & Cigoli, V. (2000). *Il famigliare. Legami, simboli e transizioni [The family core. Bonds, symbols and transitions]*. Milan: Raffaello Cortina Editore.

Scabini, E., & Galimberti, C. (1995). Adolescents and young adults: A transition in the family. *Journal of Adolescence*, *18*(5), 593–606.

Scabini, E., & Iafrate, R. (2003). *Psicologia dei legami familiari [Family bonds psychology]*. Bologna: Il Mulino.

Scabini, E., Lanz, M., & Marta, E. (1999). Psychosocial adjustment and family relationships: A typology of Italian families with a late adolescent. *Journal of Youth and Adolescence*, *28*, 633–644.

Scabini, E., & Marta, E. (1995). Family with late adolescents: Social and family topics. In M. Cusinato (Ed.), *Research on family resources and needs across the world* (pp. 177–197). Milan: LED.

Schoeni, R., & Ross, K. (2005). Material assistance from families during the transition to adulthood. In R. Settersten, F. F. Furstenberg, & R. G. Rumbaut (Eds.), *On the frontier of adulthood: Theory, research, and public policy* (pp. 396–416). Chicago, IL: University of Chicago Press.

Sciolla, L. (1993). Identità e trasmissioni dei valori: Un problema di generazioni [Identity and values transmissions: A generational issue]. In S. Ansaloni & M. Borsari (Eds.), *Adolescenti in gruppo. Costruzione dell'identità e trasmissione dei valori [Adolescents in group. Identity construction and values transmission]*. Milan: Franco Angeli.

Seginer, R. (1988a). Adolescents' orientation toward the future: Sex role differentiation in a sociocultural context. *Sex Roles, 18*(11–12), 739–757.

Seginer, R. (1988b). Social milieu and future orientation: The case of kibbutz vs. urban adolescents. *International Journal of Behavioral Development, 11*(2), 247–273.

Seginer, R. (1995). Hopes and fears of anticipated adulthood. In G. Trommsdorff (Ed.), *Kindheit und Jugend in verschienden Kulturen [Childhood and adolescence in different cultures]* (pp. 88–105). Weinheim and Munich: Juventa Verlag.

Settersten, R. A., Furstenberg, F. F., & Rumbaut, R. G. (2005). *On the frontier of adulthood: Theory, research, and public policy*. Chicago, IL: University of Chicago Press.

Sgritta, G. B. (2002). *Il gioco delle generazioni [Generations game]*. Milan: Franco Angeli.

Shek, D. T. (1997). The influence of parent–adolescent conflict on adolescent psychosocial well-being, school adjustment and problem behavior. *Social Behavior and Personality, 25*, 277–290.

Sherrod, L., Haggerty, R., & Featherman, D. (1993). Introduction: Late adolescence and the transition to adulthood. *Journal of Research on Adolescence, 3*, 217–226.

Shulman, S., & Seiffge-Krenke, I. (1997). *Fathers and adolescents. Developmental and clinical perspectives*. London: Routledge.

Skoe, E. (1988). The ethics of care. In E. Skoe & A. von der Lippe (Eds.), *Personality Development in Adolescence*. London: Routledge.

Slonim-Nevo, V., & Sheraga, Y. (1997). Social and psychological adjustment of Soviet-born and Israeli-born adolescents: The effect of the family. *Israel Journal of Psychiatry and Related Sciences, 34*(2), 128–138.

Smetana, J. G. (1995). Parenting styles and conceptions of parental authority during adolescence. *Child Development, 66*, 299–316.

Smetana, J. G., Crean, H. F., & Daddis, C. (2002). Family process and problem behaviors in middle-class African American adolescents. *Journal of Research on Adolescence, 12*(2), 275–304.

Snarey, J. (1993). *How fathers care for the next generation*. Cambridge, MA: Harvard University Press.

Snarey, J. (1998). Ego development and the ethical voices of justice and care: An Eriksonian interpretation. In P. Westenberg & A. Blasi (Eds.), *Personality development: Theoretical, empirical, and clinical investigations of Loevinger's conception of ego development* (pp. 163–180). Mahwah, NJ: Lawrence Erlbaum Associates Inc.

Sroufe, J. W. (1991). Assessment of parent–adolescent relationships: Implications for adolescent development. *Journal of Family Psychology, 5*, 21–45.

Sroufe, L., & Fleeson, J. (1988). The coherence of family relationships. In R. Hinde & J. Stevenson-Hinde (Eds.), *Relationships within the families. Mutual influences*. Oxford: Clarendon Press.

Steinberg, L., Lamborn, S. D., Dornbusch, S. M., & Darling, N. (1992). Impact of parenting practices on adolescent achievement: Authoritative parenting, school involvement, and encouragement to succeed. *Child Development, 63*(5), 1266–1281.

Steinberg, L., & Silverberg, S. B. (1986). The vicissitudes of autonomy in early adolescence. *Child Development*, *57*, 841–851.

Steinberg, S. (1987). Recent research on the family at adolescence: The extent and nature of sex differences. *Journal of Youth and Adolescence*, *16*, 191–197.

Stevens, J. P. (2002). *Applied multivariate statistics for the social sciences* (4th edn). Mahwah, NJ: Lawrence Erlbaum Associates Inc.

Stierlin, H. (1974). *Separating parents and adolescents*. New York: Quadrangle.

Stierlin, H. (1975). Countertransference in family therapy with adolescents. In M. Sugar (Ed.), *The adolescents in group and family therapy* (pp. 37–73). Oxford: Brunner/Mazel.

Straus, M. (1964). Power and support structure of the family in relation to socialization. *Journal of Marriage and the Family*, *26*(3), 318–326.

Stukas, A. A., & Dunlap, M. R. (2002). Community involvement: Theoretical approaches and educational initiatives. *Journal of Social Issues*, *58*, 411–427.

Tabachnick, B. G., & Fidell, L. S. (Eds.) (2001). *Using multivariate statistics*. Boston, MA: Allyn and Bacon.

Thomson, E., & Williams, R. (1982). Beyond wives' family sociology: A method for analyzing couple data. *Journal of Marriage and the Family*, *44*(4), 999–1008.

Toguchi Swartz, T. (2005). Transition to adulthood, personal communication.

Tonolo, G. (1999). *Adolescenza e identità [Adolescence and identity]*. Bologna: Il Mulino.

Trope, Y. (2004). Theory in social psychology: Seeing the forest and the trees. *Personality Social Psychology Review*, *8*(2), 193–200.

Uggen, C., & Janikula, J. (1999). Volunteerism and arrest in the transition to adulthood. *Social Force*, *78*(1), 331–362.

van Aken, M. A. G., Oud, J. H. L., Mathijssen, J. J. J. P., & Koot, H. M. (2001). The Social Relations Model in research on family systems. In J. R. M. Gerris (Ed.), *Dynamics of parenting* (pp. 115–130). Leuven, Belgium: Garant.

Van Wel, F., Linssen, H., & Abma, R. (2000). The parental bond and the well-being of adolescents and young adults. *Journal of Youth and Adolescence*, *29*(3), 307–318.

Vogel, J. (2002). European welfare regimes and the transition to adulthood: A comparative and longitudinal perspective. *Social Indicators Research*, *59*, 275–299.

von Bertalanffy, L., & Rapoport, A. (1960). *General systems: Yearbook of the Society for General Systems Research* (Vol. IV). Oxford: Braun-Brumfeld.

Walsh, F. (1993). *Normal family processes* (2nd edn). New York: Guilford Press.

Wapner, S., & Craig-Bray, L. (1992). Person in environment transitions: Theoretical and methodological approaches. *Environment and Behavior*, *24*(2), 161–188.

White, J. (1991). *Dynamics of family development: The theory of family development*. New York: Guilford.

White, J. (1999). Political socialization in a divided society: The case of Northern Ireland. In M. Yates & J. Youniss (Eds.), *Roots of civic identity* (pp. 156–177). Cambridge: Cambridge University Press.

Williams, P., Barclay, L., & Schmied, V. (2004). Defining social support in context: A necessary step in improving research, intervention, and practice. *Qualitative Health Research*, *14*(7), 942–960.

Wills, T. A., & Shinar, O. (2000). Measuring perceived and received social support. In S. Cohen, L. G. Underwood, & B. H. Gottlieb (Eds.), *Social support meas-*

urement and intervention. A guide for health and social scientists (pp. 86–135). New York: Oxford University Press.

Yates, M., & Youniss, J. (1996a). Community service and political-moral identity in adolescents. *Journal of Research on Adolescence, 6,* 271–284.

Yates, M., & Youniss, J. (1996b). A developmental perspective on community service in adolescence. *Social Development, 5,* 85–111.

Yates, M., & Youniss, J. (1999). *Roots of civic identity.* Cambridge: Cambridge University Press.

Youniss, J., Bales, S., Christmas-Best, V., Diversi, M., McLaughlin, M., & Silbereisen, R. (2002). Youth civic engagement in the twenty-first century. *Journal of Research on Adolescence, 12*(1), 121–148.

Youniss, J., & Ketterlinus, R. D. (1987). Communication and connectedness in mother– and father–adolescent relationships. *Journal of Youth and Adolescence, 16*(3), 265–280.

Youniss, J., & Smollar, J. (1985). *Adolescent relation with mother, father, friends.* Chicago: University of Chicago Press.

Youniss, J., & Yates, M. (1997). *Community service and social responsibility in youth.* Chicago: University of Chicago Press.

Zaccaro, S., Blair, V., Peterson, C., & Zazanis, M. (1985). Collective efficacy. In J. Maddux (Ed.), *Self-efficacy, adaptation, and adjustment: Theory, research, and application* (pp. 305–328). New York: Plenum Press.

Author index

Subject index